CHILE'S MARXIST EXPERIMENT

World Realities Series

Published
  Chile's Marxist Experiment by ROBERT MOSS

In preparation
  The War in the Sudan 1955–72 by CECIL EPRILE
  China as a World Power by W. A. C. ADIE
  North Vietnam and its Neighbours by P. J. HONEY
  Italy Since World War II by JOHN EARLE

WORLD REALITIES

Chile's Marxist Experiment

Robert Moss

DAVID & CHARLES
NEWTON ABBOT

For Hernán and Marcela who taught me
so much about patience and courage

0 7153 6415 4

© ROBERT MOSS 1973

Reprinted 1975

Printed in Great Britain by
Redwood Burn Limited
Trowbridge & Esher
for David & Charles (Holdings) Limited
South Devon House Newton Abbot Devon

Contents

Introduction

The way that Salvador Allende met his death will haunt the imagination of the left, just as it will continue to trouble those who are not sure what he stood for. Three years of Marxist rule in Chile ended in the smoking ruins of his presidential palace on 11 September 1973. His wife later said that he decided to take his own life as the soldiers who had risen against him stormed the palace. Ironically, it seems that the instrument he chose was a machine-gun once presented to him by Fidel Castro: a gift from a man who believed that a revolution cannot be made without violence to one who thought that it could—although at the last, Allende was ready to grasp at any chance of holding on to power. Allende chose death rather than exile, rejecting four separate offers of a safe conduct. He had seen the collapse of all he planned for. Maybe he felt that death was preferable to a retirement divided between a villa in Havana and speech-making over fashionable dinner-tables.

The question is, what did he die for? Did he die, as many of his well-wishers insisted, trying to defend democracy against a nasty clique of Fascist conspirators? Did he die (as his New Left critics thought) because it took him too long to realise that, in the end, you can't bring about a socialist revolution by peaceful means? Or was the action of the armed forces the desperate last resort of the opposition majority in the country which had seen the Marxists trample on their political rights and drag Chile into bankruptcy? Was it even possible that the September coup headed off a bloody and protracted civil war by destroying the bases for the Bolshevik-style insurrection that the extreme left was planning?

This book provides answers to these questions that will not be relished by those who persist in seeing Dr Allende as a benign social reformer or who imagine that because he was brought to power by a free election (though with only 36 per cent of the electorate behind him) he somehow had the right to behave as he liked during his six-year term. Nor will this book be entirely palatable to those who believe that it is a laudable aim to try to 'create a second Cuba by peaceful means'—as a respected British development economist, who should certainly have known better, once put it.

In the demonology of the left, Latin-American coups are by definition the work of the CIA, working in collusion with sinister right-wing *camarillas* devoid of popular backing. But the coup in Chile was not an everyday Latin-American *putsch*. The armed forces did not move in a political vacuum. And their decision to intervene had nothing to do with Washington. The generals tolerated Dr Allende, the world's first freely-elected Marxist ruler, for three years. They even participated in three of his cabinets. Their decision to overthrow him was taken painfully and reluctantly.

It was based on four things: (i) the objective evidence that the Allende government had plunged Chile into the worst social and economic crisis in its modern history characterised by a Weimar rate of inflation; (ii) the conviction that the Marxist parties were aiming for nothing less than the seizure of absolute power; (iii) the existence of a clear popular mandate for military intervention, demonstrated by the declarations of the Supreme Court, Congress and opposition and trade union leaders; and (iv) the discovery of the efforts of the extreme left to incite rebellion within the armed forces themselves. This last factor, as in Brazil in 1964 and in Indonesia in 1965, was what finally tipped the balance. The armed forces had to move in September, not only to save the country but to save themselves from what may well have been an impending 'night of the long knives'.

If these propositions sound somewhat extreme, it is partly because western readers were not notably well-served by the press coverage of the three years of the 'Marxist experiment' —although Allende certainly was. This book is an attempt to show what was really happening to Chile under a confetti-cloud of phrases like 'reform', 'people's government', and 'the necessary cost of building socialism'. It provides a dossier on the appalling economic legacy of the Allende government, the product not merely of incompetence but of a calculated strategy for the conquest of power. For the Marxists who surrounded Salvador Allende, the central issue was always power, not efficiency or social justice. They set out to make the Chilean revolution 'irreversible' (which, for the lay reader, means setting up a totalitarian system) by three different tactics. At the very beginning, they had some hopes of building up enough support in the country to push through a referendum on a new constitution that would do away with parliament and the existing courts. Their hopes were dashed when they narrowly failed to win a majority in the municipal elections of April 1971, in the honeymoon phase of the regime. After that, their popularity in the country fell sharply, and Allende never dared to face the voters in a plebiscite. The electoral ambitions of the left were forgotten and the emphasis was placed on other methods.

The Allende government moved at hurricane speed—often acting outside the law—to confiscate private property, in the hope that by transforming Chile's economic structures it could destroy the financial base of the opposition parties and the free press. In terms of the ownership of industry, Chile, already one of the most socialist countries in Latin America (with some 50 per cent of industrial production under state control) was turned into one of the most socialist countries outside the Communist bloc (with some 80 per cent of industrial production under state control). Whatever abstract virtues may be read into this, its effects on production were catastrophic.

Finally, a powerful section of Allende's Popular Unity

coalition (as well as the revolutionary groups outside the government) were engaged from the very beginning in preparing for a violent insurrection: a revolution within the revolution. They were helped by the foreign extremists who flooded into the country under Allende and were frequently equipped with Chilean identification papers. Some 14,000 foreign extremists involved in revolutionary activities in Chile were identified by military intelligence after the coup. The Cubans and North Koreans also played an important part in supplying Czech weapons and military instructors. During the last months of the regime, as it became obvious that Allende could no longer count on the support of the men in uniform, Communists as well as Socialists worked feverishly to prepare their armed brigades for the impending clash. Régis Debray, who saw Allende for the last time in August 1973, summed it up this way in the *Nouvel Observateur*: 'We all knew that it was merely a tactical matter of winning time to organise, to arm, to co-ordinate the military formations of the parties that made up the Popular Unity government. It was a race against the clock.' The armed forces sounded the alarm just in time, as is shown in the last chapter.

This introduction was written a few days after the coup, as the author packed his bags to go back to Santiago. The bulk of this book was written before Allende was overthrown. It cannot therefore provide a complete history of the last days of the Allende regime, although the author plans to write the inside story of the coup at a later stage. But it is an attempt to explain why the coup came about. The fall of Allende meant the temporary death of democracy in a country that had enjoyed a longer history of constitutional rule than most West-European countries. This was a tragedy for Chile, but there must be no confusion about where the responsibility lies. It lies with Dr Allende and his fellow-Marxists, who pursued their plans for the seizure of total power to the point at which the opposition despaired of restraining them by constitutional means.

Shortly before the coup, both the Supreme Court and the

Congress ruled that the government had repeatedly violated the constitution. Congress declared that 'the government is not merely responsible for isolated violations of the law and the constitution; it has made them into a permanent system of conduct' and appealed to the military to call it to order. This means that the coup has to be seen as the unconstitutional ouster of a government that had itself become unconstitutional. By abusing his executive authority to flout the views of Congress and the courts, Allende paved the way for his own downfall, since he destroyed confidence in the country's democratic institutions. The coup was acceptable to many politically-conscious civilians because a general feeling had grown up that parliament was irrelevant to the real power-struggle that was taking place. The process by which the celebrated 'democratic mentality' of the Chileans was broken down holds some sombre lessons for Europe.

Chile mattered to Europe far more than its size and eccentric geographical location would suggest. This was because it was always accepted that the process that began on 4 September 1970 (when Allende won a plurality in the presidential elections) would be a sort of test-tube experiment for the democratic societies in general. The results would show to what extent Marxism is compatible with democracy and could hardly fail to influence the politics of France and Italy. It is idle to expect any consensus on the lessons to be drawn from Chile. As the violent world reactions to the news of Allende's fall indicated, the subject has become just as emotive as the debate over the Spanish civil war, or Vietnam, or the Middle-East situation.

Those ensnared in the elaborate mythology that was woven around the Marxist regime will no doubt continue to believe, as an article of faith, that Allende went down under the slings and arrows of the CIA, the local 'feudalists', and maybe the 'rich world' in general, despite the fact that there is plenty of evidence that the coup was home-grown and widely supported. A Chilean friend of the author's who was prominent in the opposition remarked with some prescience three

months before the coup that 'If we do stop Allende, many of
the world media will say we are fascists. I don't care any more.
You reach a point where you get sick of arguing.'

His prediction was borne out by an editorial in the London
Observer (16 September 1973) that likened the Allende
regime to that of Dubcek in Czechoslovakia, and made out
that two men who had tried to give a 'human face' to
socialism had been crushed by the armoured treads of the reaction. Few comments on the coup in the western press exposed so much ignorance about conditions in Chile, or such
egregious colour-blindness. Dubcek failed in the most tragic
way to make Czechoslovakia a less conformist Soviet satellite.
The Chilean Communists, in contrast, were the first outside
the Warsaw Pact to applaud the Soviet invasion of Czechoslovakia. Far from working to give Chilean socialism a 'human
face', they were labouring to turn Chile into a submissive
Communist satellite—a kind of Latin-American Czechoslovakia. The Red Army intervened to destroy the possibility of
pluralism; the Chilean army acted to preserve it, at the cost
of the temporary loss of some basic liberties.

Chile's generals reached the conclusion that democracy
does not have the right to commit suicide. Some western
liberals, for worthy motives, believe that democrats should
stay consistent to the last: that if their system allows its
enemies the means to destroy it, they are still required to
play by their own rules. General Augusto Pinochet and his
colleagues, supported by many civilian leaders, came to see
things differently. They decided that the moment had come
when the country had to choose the lesser of two evils: either
to lapse into a uniform, and probably unalterable, form of
Marxist dictatorship; or to impose a looser, transitional form
of military rule that would allow time to restore the country
to its former ways. The Chilean generals knew perfectly well
they could offer no permanent solution for their highly complex, highly politicised, society. But, after the fighting, they
could at least offer a chance to knit together the social and
economic fabric that the Allende government had torn apart.

CHAPTER ONE

The Santiago Model

To the men who assembled in a committee room on Capitol Hill in March 1973 to inquire into the affairs of America's eighth largest company, the International Telephone and Telegraph Corporation, Chile was a long way off. For Senator Frank Church and his four colleagues, who made up the Senate Subcommittee on Multinational Corporations, what was really at stake was the behaviour of American companies abroad, the behaviour of the CIA, and the drift of President Nixon's foreign policy. At least for the one or two members of the subcommittee who bothered to turn up each day at the hearings, these were the issues that counted.

They made several discoveries that did not go unnoticed in the press, although Mr Jack Anderson, the columnist, had stolen much of their thunder by publishing a collection of memos and correspondence that ITT executives had been foolish enough to leave undestroyed a year earlier. The subcommittee established that, before the September 1970 election in Chile, ITT had intrigued to prevent Dr Salvador Allende Gossens from coming to power, and that a senior company executive had approached the CIA with the offer of $1 million to help finance a blocking operation. The offer was refused. Then came the shock of the election results on 4 September. Contrary to the expectations of the American embassy in Santiago, the Marxist candidate did manage to win a modest plurality of the votes—36 per cent—although he had a lead of less than 40,000 votes over his right-wing opponent, Jorge Alessandri. Reacting belatedly, a CIA official now came back to ITT with a contingency plan for a programme of economic disruption designed to frighten the Chilean opposition so that they would refuse to ratify the results of the poll in Congress (as is required under the Chilean constitution when the leading candidate fails to win a clear majority of the votes). This contingency plan was never acted upon.

One of the immediate effects of these disclosures was a decision by the Overseas Private Investment Corporation (OPIC), which insures private American investors against expropriation, to refuse to pay a claim presented by ITT for some $92 million, the estimated value of its investments that had been taken over by the Marxist government. It was suggested that, by its actions in Chile, the company had unnecessarily 'provoked' the new government. There was also a good deal of cluck-clucking over the revelation that the CIA had had contacts with a multinational corporation and had actually considered a programme of economic disruption in Chile—although perhaps these facts were somewhat less shocking to the far-from-uninformed members of the Senate Subcommittee than they made them out to be. Senator Church announced that he intended to introduce a bill that would make it illegal for private companies to have contacts with the CIA.

In the course of these inquiries, which tended to get confounded in the press headlines (and perhaps in the popular mind as well) with the simultaneous investigations of the Watergate affair and the general question of the use or abuse of executive authority, the problem of Chile got sunk almost without trace. It goes without saying that it is both right and proper for American legislators to concern themselves with what big companies get up to. It appears that ITT behaved rashly and irresponsibly in Chile. But Senator Church and his colleagues hardly drew breath to ask themselves whether the fears of the unfortunate ITT executives about what was likely to happen in Chile after the advent of a Marxist government had any substance. Not merely did Allende proceed to confiscate American investments; his supporters set in motion a revolutionary process that damaged the economy more seriously than any 'foreign conspiracy' might have done, eroded the country's democratic institutions, and created a climate of class hatred that made a violent confrontation seem inevitable.

But the men who conducted the Senate hearings displayed an almost complete indifference to any piece of fact that did not contribute directly to the local political debate in Washington. Much of the false naivety about foreign interest in Chilean affairs that enveloped the hearings, might, for example, have been dispelled by a single sentence that was carefully dropped by the former American ambassador to Santiago, Mr Edward Korry, shortly before the lunchbreak on the day he appeared to give evidence. Mr Korry told the subcommittee that before the 1970 election, representatives of 'all three political camps' in Chile had approached the American embassy to ask for funds. That was a minor bombshell, although perhaps few men in the committee room knew enough about Chile to realise it. As Mr Korry later recalled, 'No-one seemed to prick up his ears. For a horrible moment, I thought my words had been wasted.' His statement was, in fact, picked up by a wire service and relayed back to Santiago, where the news that representatives of Dr Allende's Popular Unity alliance (as well as spokesmen for the Christian Democrats and the Conservative *alessandristas*) had approached the Americans for electoral funds caused a small sensation in the local press. His statement was not, however, reported in the *New York Times* or the *Washington Post*, which had given the hearings front-page coverage throughout. Perhaps that was predictable.

The hearings were not really concerned with Chile, rather with a collective fit of conscience over the 'wickedness' of Americans abroad. That is also why few voices were raised to ask some of the obvious questions: What happened to Chile after 1970? Did the Marxist government really keep its promise to respect the rules of the democratic game that enabled it to come to power? Were American interests, or the interests of other western democracies, affected by what happened in Chile? Did the Chilean 'experiment' suggest that Marxism is compatible with a pluralistic society, or the reverse? Did Allende's Chile provide the Russians with a toehold on the South-American mainland?

These are some of the questions that this little book is designed to answer. It is not intended to be a complete account of the rise and fall of Salvador Allende in Chile; it is too soon to write that, and there are still too many secrets (even in a city as fond of gossip as Santiago) that remain to be revealed. It is an attempt, however, to provide a dossier on the social and economic effects of Allende's policies, and an explanation of why, in the end, the opposition was forced to use unconstitutional means to overthrow an elected president who was behaving unconstitutionally. The findings of this book will displease those who prefer to see Allende as a sort of Chilean Clement Attlee rather than as a Kerensky or (alternatively) as a Castro of the temperate zone. They will surprise those who have been led to believe the fashionable myths about Chile: that Allende's government was promoting 'necessary reform', that it was the product of an irresistible drift to the left in Chilean politics, that the opposition was led by benighted reactionaries, and that the country's present economic crisis—the worst since the Great Depression —was part of the 'necessary cost of building socialism' and aggravated by shortages due to the fact that 'people were eating better'.

Few controversial governments in small, developing countries can have been better served by their foreign sympathisers than Allende's. That may be partly because, at least in the anglophobe world, Latin America has until very recently been a minority interest among journalists, and that the relatively tiny group of specialists has contained a disproportionately high percentage of people committed to radical change. There may be nothing particularly sinister about that; Latin America, with its traditions of political violence and its brutal contrasts of wealth and poverty, is a continent that encourages—and some would say demands—a radical approach. But Chile falls outside those clumsy categories, and it is in some ways easier to understand the pattern of Chilean politics if one tries to imagine it as a kind of lost island of Europe than as an integral part of Latin America.

It is a country where the military have only figured very briefly on the political stage (notably in the confused period from 1924 to 1932), where elections have been held fairly peaceably in every scheduled year since 1932 (and there are very few European countries that can boast a similar record) and where genuine and sweeping reform has been possible through the ballot-box. It is a country where (between 1964 and 1970) the Christian Democrats attempted their 'revolution in liberty', which may not have gone far enough to satisfy the Marxist left, but radically transformed Chilean society and the whole pattern of landholding. It is a country, finally, that is sufficiently steeped in democratic ways to allow the accession to power of a Marxist president representing barely more than a third of the electorate. Much has been made of the various schemes that were hatched to stop Allende coming to power (and notably of ITT's wild-goose chase among opposition groups) but perhaps there is no other country in Latin America where the outgoing president, and his armed forces, would have tolerated the transfer of power to a Marxist at the head of a coalition dominated by Communists and Socialists.

These are some of the reasons why Chile is 'different', and the Latin-American stereotypes fail to apply. It is not a society where a feudal oligarchy perches on the backs of the toiling peasantry like so many Old Men of the Sea. But there was one sense in which Chile could never manage to break out of Latin America. Its high degree of political and social development was not matched by any corresponding economic development, although the per capita income is relatively high. Both of the governments that preceded Allende failed to find any solution for the chronic problems of high

B

inflation and a sluggish growth rate. To orthodox Marxists and to many of the bright young men turned out by the United Nations Economic Commission for Latin America (ECLA), there was a panacea for those problems ready to hand; it all depended on changing social structures, and above all on redistributing land and income in order to increase the internal market. It was also necessary, they argued, to chase away foreign investors who were busy exploiting the country by shipping its minerals abroad and sending home profits that, over several years, were vastly in excess of their starting capital. According to Allende's apologists, this was the broad rationale for the way the government proceeded to deal with the economy.

The persistent claim that this was eventually going to result in higher production and lower inflation started to look a little threadbare, however, as time went on and the rate of inflation climbed to the Weimar level of 350 per cent over the twelve months before Allende was overthrown; the shops were emptied; and the failure of agricultural production after the confiscation of private farms made it necessary to introduce a system of rationing. If Allende could not succeed in managing the economy, could he succeed in anything else? His most persistent apologists fell back on another argument: all these reverses were part of the 'necessary cost' of building socialism. Few people, apart from the Chileans being shunted down the rocky road to socialism, appeared to ask themselves what this socialist Ithaca was, or whether the journey to it was worth the pain it entailed.

It turned out that Allende was curiously uninterested in the new concepts of socialism circulating in the west; the idea of workers' self-management, for example, apparently left him cold. When it came to running expropriated businesses, his government fell back on the most outmoded Stalinist model of state capitalism. When it came to running the lands that were confiscated—legally or illegally—at a rate that made farmers cry out that Allende's first agriculture minister was 'to private property what the tiger is to the gazelle', the Marxists were not interested in giving the land to the tiller; peasants were drafted for service on state-run farms under the eye of government bureaucrats.

None of this, perhaps, should have been surprising. It was clear to those who bothered to read the statements of the Marxist leaders themselves that Chile's Communists and Socialists were not basically aiming for social reform, or for higher production and improved efficiency in industry. They were concerned with power, which Lenin rightly defined as the basic problem of a socialist revolution.

The success of the presidential candidate of a Marxist-led coalition in 1970 surprised many of Allende's own supporters, notably in the socialist left, which had never had much faith in the prospect of revolution via the ballot-box. It was a triumph for the 'united front' tactics favoured by the Russians, who did not hesitate to stress its significance for other countries. Thus one Soviet commentator declared that Allende's victory had punctured the belief, widely held by 'ultra-leftists', that 'truly democratic forces' cannot achieve power by peaceful means.[1] It was after all something new in the world, the first occasion when a Marxist government had been freely elected. It was the first time that Karl Marx's cautious suggestion, at an Amsterdam conference in 1872, that 'the workers might attain their ends by peaceful means' had been borne out by events—though he thought that could only happen in England and America and just possibly, 'if I knew more about your institutions', in Holland.[2] The Santiago model had an obvious relevance for both France and Italy, where large Communist parties existed, and a Socialist–Communist–Radical left alliance was actually formed in Paris to contest the 1973 elections. In a broader sense, Allende's success could be used as an example of the need for Communist parties to be flexible in their tactics and their choice of allies. After all, had not Lenin himself written that 'the task of a truly revolutionary party is not to declare that it is impossible to renounce all compromises, but to be able, through all compromises, to remain true to its principles, to its class, to its revolutionary purpose'.[3]

Allende himself was very conscious of being in some sense a trailblazer. Chile was not to be a second Russia or a second Cuba; it offered a new model for 'the transition to socialism' —one of the favourite official euphemisms. Allende had this to say in his first message to Congress on 21 May 1971:

> Our revolution will follow a pluralist model, which Marxist ideologists have been able to visualise, but which they have never been able to turn into practice. Chile is the first nation upon earth that has been called upon to apply the second model for the transition to socialism. I am sure that we will have the energy and the capacity to create the first socialist society that will bring together the three ideals of liberation, democracy and a multi-party system.[4]

How those ideals were actually served by the Allende government is the basic theme of this book. Both Allende and the Communist leader, Luis Corvalán, made many formal protestations that they would respect the idea of political pluralism in Chile. In an important interview on the day that Allende took power, for example, Corvalán declared that 'the existence of just one party does not form a part of Communist principles'.[5] That statement was not entirely reassuring, since Corvalán went on to discuss how more than one party had been tolerated at the start of the Bolshevik and Cuban revolutions, neither of which resulted in a showpiece example of political pluralism. It is even more significant that, barely two years later, in a long interview with a leading Communist journalist, Corvalán was unable to give a definite assurance that his party would respect the results of the next presidential election if an opposition candidate won, and declared that he would like to outlaw several opposition newspapers.[6]

The point is that neither the Socialists nor the Communists in Chile wasted time debating the abstract virtues of a constitutional system that both rejected as 'bourgeois democracy'.

In Marxist jargon, terms like 'democracy' and 'pluralism' mean something different from what they mean in normal discourse (and it needs to be stressed that, like the Communists and unlike their European namesakes, the Chilean Socialists are Marxist–Leninists). Allende made it plain from the beginning that he wished to establish a new Constitution, in which the Senate would be abolished and Congress replaced by a 'people's assembly' elected on a new basis. The existing judicial system (the instrument of 'class justice', according to Marxist spokesmen) would give way to a network of 'popular tribunals' chosen in each neighbourhood. The fact that Allende had to work with a hostile majority in Congress meant that he was always unable to turn these projects into law. The fact that, over the same period, he was unable to convert the 36 per cent of the votes he attracted in 1970 into a majority meant that he was also unable to carry out his threats to call for a plebiscite on his plans for a new Constitution.[7] His government never enjoyed majority support although this did not stop him from by-passing Congress at the courts through the abuse of his executive powers.

Allende's avowed goals meant that formal assurances that the Marxists would continue to respect the rules of the system that had given them power could not be taken at face value. The 'Statute of Guarantees' for democratic freedoms that Allende concluded with the Christian Democratic Party before taking office proved to be no guarantee for anything. Allende made that clear enough soon after he was safely inside the La Moneda palace. Assurances of this kind, he told Régis Debray, were merely 'a tactical necessity'. At the end of 1970, 'the important thing was to take power'.[8]

There were alarming signs of the real intentions of the Marxist parties from the very beginning. The 'Statute of Guarantees' contained a pledge that the new government would respect the freedom of the press. But at the end of November 1970—a few weeks after Allende was inaugurated —pro-government journalists staged a seminar on 'Social Responsibility in the Mass Media'. At this conference, the

Communist labour leader (later to become minister of labour) Luis Figueroa delivered himself of the opinion that there can be 'real liberty of expression' only in a society in which all means of communication were controlled by the state. The Communist sociologist, Patricio Saavedra, added the view that the ideal model was provided by the Soviet Union, 'where news is published only when the public is mature enough to receive it; thus, instead of being merchandise, news becomes an instrument of political education'.[9] If these were the prospects for the press, the prospects for the country's legal institutions—another vital safeguard of the Chilean democratic system—were hardly more promising. Eduardo Novoa Monreal, who was to become Allende's chief legal adviser (and infinitely more adept than anyone in the White House at widening the scope of executive authority without reference to Congress) attacked the Chilean courts as the relics of an obsolete social and economic system. Novoa insisted that 'bourgeois law' was the product of an attempt 'to uphold in power indefinitely the political, social and economic system of liberal individualism'.[10] There was no such thing as 'the rule of law'; there was only class rule, and as the balance of social forces changed, the 'superstructures' of law, education, the media—and the parliamentary system also—would have to change accordingly. Again, there was nothing novel in this. It was a perfectly orthodox Marxist view of society. It was also a prescription for action.

For the Marxists within the new coalition, if not for all of their non-Marxist allies, the central problem after November 1970 was how to transform the capture of the government into the capture of total political power. The Socialists, in their congress at La Serena in January 1971, put it this way: 'The electoral triumph of Comrade Allende...has generated new and favourable conditions for the working class and the Chilean masses to undertake an *effective* conquest of power that will make it possible to start building socialism in this country.'[11] There was considerable disagreement within the Popular Unity alliance about how this was actually going to be brought about. The battle-lines were never rigidly fixed, but the basic rift over tactics was between the Communists and the Socialist left.

The Communists championed the view that the government should set out to consolidate its power by the means that originally enabled it to take power: by a 'centralist' strategy designed to win over sections of liberal opinion (and above all, the left wing of the Christian Democrats) and to keep the opposition divided. Simultaneously, the Communists set out to tighten their grip over the country by taking control of the economy. This meant the state takeover of farms, banks and factories without reference to Congress; and also the use of price and wage controls and eventually of rationing as well as a means of controlling the daily lives of ordinary people.

The nationalisation process gathered speed rapidly after Allende took office. By the end of his first two years, an estimated 80 per cent of industrial production was state controlled, and 75 per cent of the agricultural land had been brought within the so-called 'reformed area'. This was part of a political, rather than an economic, strategy. This process was designed to erode the economic power-base of the opposition parties and to drive the independent press towards bankruptcy by destroying its sources of finance. It was also designed to reduce the autonomy of trade unions and workers' organisations by turning most of the country's workforce into state employees, grouped within a trade union federation whose president was a Communist and ultimately responsible to a Communist minister of labour. Eventually, in accordance with sound Communist precedent, the two offices were combined. The Chilean Communists, great believers in 'social discipline', wanted to see all workers' and communal organisations subjected to a tight central control. In this they differed from the Socialist left, which had greater faith in 'spontaneity'.

These Communist tactics allowed for great flexibility. It was the Communists, for example, who were the chief advocates of bringing the army into the cabinet during two serious political crises in 1972—and they actually succeeded, that November, in drawing the armed forces into a curious, though short-lived, coalition of Marxists and military. They were relentless critics of the 'ultras' on the revolutionary left who refused to accept a tactical alliance with 'bourgeois' parties or with the military, and whose violent provocations (the Communists believed) might provide the opposition with a pretext for counter-revolution.[12] The attitudes of the Communists were shared by the Radical Party and some of the smaller non-Marxist groups that made up Popular Unity. Allende's own supporters in his faction-ridden Socialist Party tended to take a very similar line, although Allende was visibly torn during the later conflict between the Communists and the Socialist left, and on several important occasions gave in to the wild men of his own party.

An alternative strategy was advocated by the left wing of the Socialist Party, headed by Carlos Altamirano. Both left-wing Socialists, and the would-be guerrillas of the Movement of the Revolutionary Left (MIR), which remained outside the government, believed that civil war in Chile was inevitable and that the role of the left was to prepare for armed insurrection. They aimed to bring about the classical pre-revolutionary situation of 'dual power' by building up militant organisations inside state-run industries, in the workers' suburbs of Santiago, and among peasant groups. The members of these 'soviets' were to be trained and organised for a violent insurrection in which Santiago's vital services would be crippled and the industrial suburbs and revolutionary *campamentos* would 'encircle' the capital. The ultras were also agreed that, in the short term, they should aim to speed up the pace of revolutionary change by pushing the government beyond 'bourgeois legality'. This meant, in particular, the illegal and often violent seizure of farms and factories and the attempt to establish 'liberated zones' in the southern provinces and in the workers' suburbs of Santiago. As the conflict between the 'ultra-leftists' and the Communists within the Popular

Unity alliance developed, the radical Catholic groups (the Movement of United Popular Action, or MAPU, and later *Izquierda Cristiana*) tended to take sides with the Socialist left.

Allende's own position as *el señor presidente*, the man straddling the entire coalition, was rather ambiguous. He let the Communists have their way in running the economy, especially after his first minister of economy, Pedro Vuskovic, was dropped in June 1972. He followed their advice on co-opting the military and attempting to maintain a dialogue with the opposition Christian Democrats. On the other hand, he was prepared to make a series of important concessions to the ultras and refused to take firm action against the paramilitary groups on the extreme left who were actively and openly preparing for an armed uprising. He always kept a foot in both camps.

Many foreigners who knew him found it hard to imagine this middle-aged party professional as a genuine revolutionary. They were more impressed by his taste for the good life— evident in his carefully-tailored clothes, his expensively-furnished houses, and his penchant for good food and drink and attractive women—and by his studied diplomacy, his celebrated *muñeca*, as the Chileans call it. Could this arrogant, affable Freemason, with forty years' experience of parliamentary politics, really be a convinced Marxist bent upon destroying his country's political system? Few people thought of Allende as a political heavyweight. He was a brilliant political manipulator, a master of the art of divide and rule, of playing one man off against another. He vastly enjoyed the office of president, and no doubt his main concern after he entered La Moneda was to stay there, at least until the end of his six-year term. This led people to believe that, if he were forced to choose between staying in power with the support of the military at the price of suppressing the ultra-left and gambling on the chance of holding the left together despite the risk of an emerging civil war situation, he would choose the first option. That did not happen. Allende was given many chances to turn back, to make the break with the ultras—his refusal led to his tragic death. Instead he allowed them to build the huge stockpiles of arms uncovered after the coup and to carry their preparations for an uprising to the point where the military had to step in. This is by no means clear. In the short term, Allende had been ready to work with almost everyone; but there is some reason to think that, at the end of his first two and a half years, he had made the unity of the left his prime target, at the cost of new concessions to the ultras that hardened the battle-lines in Chile.

Allende was not an original political thinker, and understood nothing of economics. But he was a lifelong Marxist whose youthful Trotskyism had not been diluted by all his years on a Senate bench. Perhaps even more important, his immediate family contained several prominent members of the revolutionary left. His sister, Laura Allende, was a Sociaist deputy close to Carlos Altamirano. His nephew, Andres Pascal Allende, was one of the leaders of the Movement of the Revolutionary Left (MIR) and edited one of its journals. His daughter, 'Tati', was married to a senior member of the Cuban embassy, Louis de Oña, who was the desk officer in Havana responsible for co-ordinating Che Guevara's expedition to Bolivia. A man inherits his family, but chooses his friends. These family details might count for less if Allende had not chosen to surround himself with young militants from the MIR and the Socialist left, who formed his private body-guard (*Grupo de Amigos Personales del Presidente*) and intelligence service. Some Chileans believed that, in a literal sense, he became their prisoner—and that their physical presence made it impossible for him to take any strong action against the revolutionary left without endangering his own life. This may have been part of the reason why Allende tried to prevent the conflict within the Marxist left from tearing his coalition apart. It is also true that, if in an intellectual sense Allende might be regarded as a Communist, in an emotional sense he remained committed to his own Socialist Party, which was anti-Communist in its origins. While, in the short term, the clash between the New Left and the orthodox Marxists seriously weakened the government, Allende himself may have believed that, in the long term, the two tactics of the Marxist left were not entirely compatible, and that if a civil war situation emerged, the Communists, Socialists and *miristas* would have to pool their resources.

The conflict between the Marxists and the opposition parties took place on three different fronts. There was the political contest between the president and Congress, in which the opposition majority in the legislature was shown to be incapable of imposing constraints on the government's policy, although this was because rifts in the opposition initially prevented it from using all of its parliamentary options. There was the fight for control of the economy, the real key —in the eyes of the Marxists themselves—to seizing total political power. And finally, there was the looming conflict for control of the streets. One of the most depressing side-effects of the way that Congress was by-passed by the government was that both sides became increasingly convinced that the final outcome in Chile would be decided by extra-parliamentary forms of action. The extremists took that to mean revolutionary (or counter-revolutionary) violence; union and student leaders took it to mean strike action and massive demonstrations. Perhaps the Marxists were better prepared for this confrontation, at least at the outset; they had fewer scruples about the constitution.

The history of Chile between November 1970 and September 1973 can be divided into five main phases.[13] The *first phase*, from Allende's accession to power until the Arrayán conference of the Popular Unity parties in January 1972, was a period of rapid nationalisation of farms and factories, and radical redistribution of income. The results of the municipal elections in April 1971, in which Allende's supporters managed to win nearly half of the votes, were a tremendous fillip for the new government—even though it was pointed out that the results were only to be expected during the 'honeymoon phase' of a new regime. Over most of this period, the opposition remained divided and at odds with itself. During this phase, it was shown that (because of the wide-ranging executive powers of the Chilean presidency and because Allende's legal advisers were able to exploit little-known existing laws) Congress and the courts were powerless to block the revolutionary process. But by the end of the period—partly as a result of the example of spontaneous pro-test movements like the housewives' march in Santiago in December 1971—a tactical alliance had been forged between the Christian Democrat and National parties and attempts were made to impeach individual ministers. By the end of the first phase, the Allende government had to contend with a, number of serious problems: on the economic front, with rapidly rising inflation, falling production and acute shortages of basic food and consumer goods; on the political front, with the new militancy of the opposition—which had been unable to use its parliamentary majority to block the Marxist pro-gramme, with rising political violence, starting with the murder of a former Christian Democratic minister in June 1971, and with the now-open rift within the ruling alliance. The government's loss of popularity was demonstrated by the results of the by-elections in January 1972, and the upshot was a self-criticism session in a house in El Arrayán, outside Santiago.

The *second phase,* from January to June 1972, was a period of accentuated conflict within the Popular Unity coalition. The debate centred on whether the government should draw breath to consolidate its gains, or should press ahead with further expropriations without concern for the economic effects. The founding of a 'people's assembly' by the MIR, the Socialist left and the radical Catholics in Concepción in May was a direct challenge to the 'centrists' in the government. But at the end of this phase, in the conference at Lo Curro in June that led to the formation of a new cabinet, it was the 'centrist' line of the Communists that won out. Pedro Vuskovic, the main architect of the government's economic policy, was dropped from the cabinet, and Orlando Millas, a

Communist whose innate caution and open contempt for the would-be guerrillas of the extreme left (and for Fidel Castro) had earned him the hatred of many young Socialists, was brought in as finance minister.

During the *third phase*, up till the formation of a new cabinet in November, the government failed to halt the continued deterioration of the economy. Allende had inherited foreign reserves worth $400 million from the previous government; by the end of June 1972, there was a *negative* balance of $28 million.[14] It was during this phase that Allende again tried, unsuccessfully, to fracture the embryonic opposition alliance by making new overtures to the Christian Democrats. His overtures failed. Popular reactions to the worsening economic situation, the fears of shopkeepers and small businessmen at having their firms taken away, and the general frustration of opposition groups at their incapacity to apply the brakes to the revolutionary process by parliamentary means or appeal to the courts were all vented in the strike movement of October. The two key groups that initiated the strike—the truckdrivers and shopkeepers—remained on strike for twenty-seven days and presented Allende with the gravest political crisis of his first two years.

The final outcome was a dramatically different kind of government—a 'civil–military cabinet' in which three military ministers took their seats alongside Communists and Socialists. From 2 November 1972, when the military joined the government, until 22 March 1973, when they dropped out, it might have been said that a Marxist president was kept in power by the bayonets of the armed forces. This was the *fourth phase*, during which the opposition devoted most of its efforts to electoral campaigning in preparation for the 4 March legislative elections. Allende's followers scored surprisingly well, although there was later evidence of a massive government fraud. A headline in the left-wing daily *Puro Chile* on the morning after the results were announced read 'The People: 43%. The Reactionaries: 55%'.

When the 'reactionaries' (*momios*) constitute a clear majority of the electorate, perhaps they deserve a more flattering name. The election results showed that Allende had failed to win majority support for a policy that had radically transformed Chile's social and economic structures and eroded its legal and parliamentary institutions. They also showed, however, that the Marxist parties had had considerable success in building up its constituency in working-class urban areas, and in winning new support in the provinces—where shortages of food were not yet as acute as in the towns.

The *final phase* of the Marxist experiment began when the military ministers left the cabinet on 28 March. Against the background of rising violence and the deepening economic crisis, Allende sought vainly for a new formula for government. He was driven back to an old one: the Marxist–military alliance. General Prats, now deeply compromised with the regime, was able to persuade his less enthusiastic colleagues in the high command to participate in a new joint cabinet. But it collapsed after less than a fortnight and shortly afterwards the high command forced Prats to resign as commander-in-chief.

This brought about a sea-change in Chilean politics. Under the new commander-in-chief, General Pinochet, the anti-Marxist generals were able to press ahead with plans for military intervention. When they finally moved against Allende, however, they did not move in a political vacuum. They moved only after the Supreme Court and Congress had both declared that the government had violated the constitution. They moved after it had long been clear that the extreme left was promoting subversion within the barracks as well as among civilian groups. They moved when it had become obvious that the opposition majority in the country had failed to curb the Marxists by peaceful means, and that Chile's democratic institutions had been made tragically irrelevant to the real power-struggle that was under way.

Notes to this chapter are on page 206

CHAPTER TWO

Revolution by Ballot

Why was Allende elected? It might be argued that his victory was a product of popular frustration with the government of President Eduardo Frei (1964–70), which had encouraged hopes and revolutionary demands that it was unable or unwilling to satisfy. The Christian Democrats had fallen into the familiar trap of all liberal reformers, and found themselves, at the end of Frei's 'revolution in liberty', uncomfortably sandwiched between those who wanted to grab more and those who wanted to give away less. The last year of Frei's government was a confused period of street violence, protest marches, rising unemployment and steep inflation. It saw the first nationwide strike by peasants and farm labourers, who called for a more radical programme of land redistribution. It also saw a one-day general strike ordered by the Communist-dominated trade union federation (CUT) in June in support of Allende.

But these labour troubles should not be taken as a sign of a significant swing to the left in Chilean politics. Voting figures show that the real swing was the other way. It is a remarkable fact that Allende was elected with a smaller share of the votes than the forces that made up his Popular Unity coalition had managed to attract at the two previous presidential elections. In 1958, the political groups that later backed the Popular Unity alliance managed to get 43.9 per cent of the votes. In 1964, in competition with Frei, they could claim only 38.7 per cent of the votes. And on 4 September 1970, Allende's share of the poll dropped to 36.3 per cent.

Allende did not win because Chilean voters had moved to the left. He won in spite of the fact that nearly two-thirds of the electorate voted against him. The reason is simple. His opponents were divided. The conservatives were not prepared to back a Christian Democrat candidate, Radomiro Tomic, whose programme seemed alarmingly similar to that of the Marxists. And for their part, the Christian Democrats chose to tolerate a Marxist government rather than side with the right-wing supporters of Jorge Alessandri.

At the previous presidential election in 1964, the Chilean voters had been offered a choice between two basic alternatives: Frei or Allende. The third candidate, the Radical Julio Durán (later the leader of the Radical Democrats) did not stand a chance after the right-wing Conservative and Liberal parties withdrew their support. Both Frei and Allende promised reform, but Frei had the additional advantage of support from the traditional right-wing parties. After the shock of the Curicó by-election early in 1964, the Liberal and Conservative parties (which later merged to form the National Party) decided to withdraw Julio Durán as their presidential candidate and transfer their backing to Frei. In Curicó, a Marxist had managed to win what had always been regarded as a conservative safe seat. The conservative leaders were flexible enough to bury their quarrel with the Christian Democrats temporarily in order to remove the possibility that a Marxist government might profit from it and thus win an electoral plurality. The result was a sweeping electoral victory for Frei in which he was able to obtain the first absolute majority that a presidential candidate had won in recent Chilean history.

In 1970, however, the Chilean electorate was offered three alternatives: Allende on the left, Alessandri on the right and Radomiro Tomic on the Christian Democrat ticket. This time there was no real possibility that the conservative forces would agree to support the Christian Democrat candidate, partly because—on the evidence of their dramatic resurgence during the second half of the Frei administration—they were confident of winning the election themselves, and partly because Tomic seemed to represent many of the same things as Allende. In retrospect, it is not easy to understand why the Christian Democrats chose Tomic. He was long regarded as Frei's special protégé, but on his return from a period as ambassador in Washington in 1968, he aligned himself with the radical wing of the Christian Democratic Party, in opposition to the Conservative group centred round Frei's finance minister, Andrés Zaldivar, and his minister of the interior, Pérez Zujovic.

While Tomic remained within the party after a faction that advocated open alliance with the Marxists broke away in 1969, he entered into close negotiations with the Communists and was at one stage considered as a possible presidential candidate for a Marxist–Christian Democrat alliance. He had made a notorious speech early in 1969 in which he declared he would not run as the candidate for an 'isolated' Christian Democratic Party, although these words were quickly forgotten and he was formally nominated in August that year.

In his electoral campaign, Tomic called for the 'deepening' of the existing reform programme and the more rapid pursuit of a 'non-capitalist process of development'. Many of his demands for faster redistribution of land and for nationalisation of foreign economic interests were indistinguishable from the programme of the Popular Unity coalition, but it was not realised until after the election how closely he had identified himself with the left-wing parties.

It later transpired that, before the election was held, Tomic entered into a secret agreement with Allende to the effect that if one of them got a majority of 30,000 votes or more over the runner-up, the other would publicly recognise his victory. The existence of this pact only became known after the election, although Tomic never publicly admitted to its existence. It seems that there was, in effect, an agreement to commit the Christian Democratic bloc in Congress to vote for Allende if he received a relative majority in the

c

election.[1] (Under the Chilean constitution, it is the role of Congress to choose between the two leading contenders in a presidential election where no one obtains an absolute majority.)

The leaders of the conservative National Party[2] did not see Tomic as a genuine alternative to Allende. They were also confident of their own electoral chances, as was the American embassy in Santiago. Ambassador Korry prophesied a narrow victory for Alessandri in his despatches to Washington. As it turned out, his statistics were not far wrong—except that the respective positions of Allende and Alessandri were reversed. The right had gathered strength as the reaction to the Christian Democrats' reform programme set in. In 1965, the Liberal and Conservative parties together had only been able to attract 12.8 per cent of the votes in the congressional elections. Campaigning together as the National Party in the municipal elections of 1967, they were able to increase their share of the vote to 14.6 per cent. And in the congressional elections of 1969, the figure rose to 20.8 per cent.

In preparing to contest the 1970 election, the Nationals set out to broaden their appeal by choosing a populist candidate with a 'supra-party' image. Jorge Alessandri, the son of Arturo Alessandri, the reformist *caudillo* of the 1930s, finally accepted nomination in November 1969. He declared that his mission was 'to unite all the Chileans without distinction of party or political ambition' and in their manifestoes, the Nationals insisted on the need to 'substitute national feeling for class conflict'.[3]

But Alessandri was 73 years old, and a bachelor, and he was rapidly subjected to a campaign of personal abuse by the left-wing press that was only equalled by the later campaign of vilification against Frei during the run-up to the March 1973 legislative elections. The left-wing daily *Clarín* distinguished itself by dubbing him 'La Señora'.[4] His campaign tours around the countryside were systematically disrupted by Popular Unity sympathisers and the 15,000-odd *comités de Unidad Popular* set up to support Allende and secure 'popular participation' in the work of government after his election. But it was probably television that did most to destroy Alessandri, just as it helped to destroy Richard Nixon in 1960. The cameras showed him up as an old man, visibly fading. The man could no longer quite match the name.

All the same, the election was a close-run thing. The results were as follows:

Allende	1,070,334	36.3 per cent
Alessandri	1,031,151	34.98 per cent
Tomic	821,000	27.84 per cent

So much for Tomic's promise in 1964 that the Christian Democrats would rule Chile for at least thirty years.

But the election results were not enough to secure Allende's victory. Under the terms of the constitution, the final decision rested with Congress. Counting deputies and senators together, Allende could count on 80 votes in Congress, the Christian Democrats could muster 75, and Alessandri's supporters totalled 45. These figures meant that Allende either had to persuade the Christian Democratic Party to support him, or persuade Tomic's followers to defect. Since Radomiro Tomic had rushed to Allende's house shortly after his victory had been announced to offer his congratulations, it may have seemed that a favourable vote for Allende in Congress was a foregone conclusion. But Allende predicted that in the period between 4 September and 4 November—when the new president was due to be inaugurated—'Chile was going to feel like a football being kicked around by a Pele.' And he was right.

It was a tremendous turning-point. The world had not yet seen a society that had peacefully accepted the assumption of power by a Marxist government, and many of Allende's supporters were sceptical about whether they would actually be permitted to enter the Moneda palace.

As soon as the election results were known, there was panic among private investors. On the first day that people could get into the banks (Monday, 7 September) 180 million escu-

dos were withdrawn from private deposits. By the following
Wednesday, the amount withdrawn rose to some 650 million
escudos. Andrés Zaldivar, the finance minister, appeared on
television and made a statement in which he outlined the
dangerous effects that the new climate of uncertainty had had
on the economy. In his interview with Régis Debray, Allende
later professed to see in the financial panic 'the first stage of
a conspiracy' designed to prevent him taking office.[5] The
documents from the private files of the International Telephone and Telegraph Corporation (ITT) made public by
the American columnist Jack Anderson early in 1972 gave
Allende some useful—if belated—evidence to support these
allegations, and they were duly reprinted in a handsome edition by a state publishing house.[6]

The ITT papers did show that at least one powerful foreign
corporation had been sufficiently alarmed by the prospect of
a Marxist government in Chile to offer funds for use by
the opposition and to lobby for preventive action by the
American government. ITT's local representatives also made
advances to other American companies active in Chile to
discuss the prospects for 'economic disruption', but failed to
find any takers. Most important, some of ITT's men seem to
have acted as 'scouts' among the armed forces and the opposition politicians. They found that General Roberto Viaux,
who had engineered a mutiny by the Tacna regiment in
support of pay demands the previous year, was 'gung-ho to
move immediately'.

But Viaux had little sense of timing, and was completely
out of tune with his commander-in-chief, General René
Schneider, who threatened to have him shot if he acted on his
own account. The ITT men noted that he failed to enlist
the support of 'any key troop commanders, at least to our
knowledge'.[7]

The ITT scouts were even more disappointed with President Frei's personal attitude. In one report, an ITT vice-
president wrote that 'All past evaluations of Frei's weaknesses
in a crisis are now being confirmed. Worse, it has been estab-

lished beyond any doubt that he has been double-dealing to preserve his own stature and image as the champion of Latin American democracy. For instance: he told some of his Ministers he would be quite willing to be removed by a military coup. This would absolve him from any involvement in a coup that would, in turn, upset Allende. Then, he turned right round and told the military chiefs that he was totally against a coup.'[8]

The ITT papers clearly showed that one American corporation had strayed into politics to the extent of casting itself in the role of a foreign policy adviser to the White House and attempting to consolidate a Chilean opposition movement capable of blocking Allende's succession to power. They were later used as a pretext for the confiscation of ITT's Chilean assets. The ITT papers did not, on the other hand, provide any clear guide to the labyrinthine intrigues that went on in Santiago during the fifty days between the September election and the vote in Congress on 24 October. Nor did they implicate President Frei or any government minister in those intrigues.

It is still hard to sort out the truth behind all the allegations that were put forward by the Popular Unity press. Bands of right-wing extremists did plant bombs and provoke street disorders in the attempt to create the climate of violence in which the army might intervene. But the most plausible attempt to block Allende in the immediate aftermath of the election was a purely political move. On 9 September, Alessandri put forward his own plan. He promised to resign immediately if he were elected by Congress, in order to allow new presidential elections to be held in which he would not stand as a candidate. As it turned out, his proposals were never seriously considered.

On 13 September, Allende warned that the country would be paralysed by strikes and violent land seizures if Congress failed to confirm his election. And on 24 September, the Christian Democrats presented their own plan. They would consider supporting Allende if the Popular Unity coalition

would agree to a 'Statute of Guarantees' designed to preserve
democratic freedoms—in particular, the freedom of the press,
the trade unions and the universities, the autonomy of the
armed forces, and the preservation of the traditional distinction between the legislature, the executive and the judiciary.
Allende refused to accept any curbs on his power to appoint
the commander-in-chief of the armed forces, but the statute
was approved in a modified form by the chamber of deputies on 15 October. When it was accepted by the senate four
days later, Alessandri decided to withdraw his candidacy.

The real turning-point had come on 3 October, when 271
out of the 500 delegates at an extraordinary meeting of the
Christian Democratic Party voted to support Allende. The
Statute of Guarantees was essentially a sop to the doubters
within the party, and few people appeared to notice that it
failed to mention the right of property. Allende always held
a trump card in his dealings with the Christian Democrats;
the fact that he could count on between 20 and 25 Christian
Democratic left-wingers to back him if the party as a whole refused. After the Statute of Guarantees was accepted, Allende's
election by Congress seemed a foregone conclusion. But there
was one more hurdle to be jumped.

Just forty-eight hours before the final vote, at 8.30 on the
morning of 22 October, Schneider's car was ambushed as
he drove to the office. He was surrounded by a group of
young men and shot as he tried to remove a revolver from his
briefcase. He died three days later. Since five of his assailants
managed to flee the country, it is difficult to ascertain the full
truth surrounding the Schneider killing. Much of the evidence, significantly, came from the Movement of the Revolutionary Left (MIR) one of whose leaders, Luciano Cruz,
had made it his mission to infiltrate the right-wing circle
around General Roberto Viaux.[9]

It seems that Viaux's supporters had evolved a scheme to
kidnap the commander-in-chief and provide the pretext for a
military coup by making the abduction appear the work of
the extreme left.[10] A number of senior officers, including

Admiral Tirado Barros, the navy commander, General Vale-
zuela Godoy, the chief of the Santiago garrison, and Vincente
Huerta Celis, the director of the Carabineros, were allegedly
involved in the plot.

Schneider was chosen as the target because of his reputation as a 'constitutional' general devoted to keeping the army
out of politics. Earlier in the year, he had sent a letter to *El
Mercurio* in which he declared that the army was the
'guarantee of a normal election and of the assumption of
power by whoever is elected by the people, either by an absolute majority or by the joint houses of Congress in the event
that no candidate gets more than 50 per cent of the votes'.[11]
In the eyes of some conservative officers, Schneider's politics
were suspect since two of his four sons had actively cam-
paigned for Allende's election.

Whatever Schneider's assailants actually intended, it is
highly improbable that their plans involved blood-letting.
His death must have been either the result of panic; or (as
some observers believed possible) the work of a *mirista* agent
provocateur planted inside the kidnap group. The 'special
group' formed to carry out the abduction included some very
ambiguous characters like the mercenary 'Severino' as well
as the scions of some of Chile's wealthiest families,[12] and it
would not have been too difficult to infiltrate an MIR agent,
given the notorious indiscretion of some of the leading conspirators. The *mirista* leader, Luciano Cruz, was in close con-
tact with the Viaux circle in the weeks before the kidnapping.

At any rate, the death of General Schneider inspired a
general mood of shock and revulsion among the Chilean
public. Chile had not witnessed a political assassination since
the murder of Diego Portales, the founder of the 'autocratic
republic' in 1833. The government proclaimed a state of
siege, and a retired general was placed in charge of the public
inquiry into the assassination. The murder of the commander-
in-chief put paid to any last-gasp hopes of blocking Allende's
accession to power, and it secured the neutrality of the armed
forces. The Congress vote duly took place on 24 October, and

the Christian Democrats voted to recognise Allende's victory. He took possession of La Moneda, the dust-coloured and somewhat dreary presidential palace, on 4 November.

Popular Fronts in Chile

Before looking at the curious combination of forces that carried Allende to power, it is useful to glance backwards at Chile's earlier experiment in government by a popular front. Chile was one of the first testing-grounds (with France and Spain) for Communist popular front tactics in the 1930s. The country experienced three successive popular front governments in the decade after 1938 under three presidents drawn from the Radical Party: Pedro Aguirre Cerda (1938–42); Juan Antonio Rios (1942–6); and Gabriel Gonzalez Videla (1946–52). This was a period of rapid change in Chile, with the creation of new heavy industries, the widening of the role of the state in the economy, and the introduction of important social reforms. But in retrospect, it was a somewhat inglorious time for the Marxist parties. The Socialists' initial threat to introduce 'a socialist economic system in which private property will become collectivised' and establish a 'dictatorship of the proletariat'[13] came to nothing and the middle-class Radicals stayed securely in the saddle. The Communists, far from becoming the dominant partner in the coalition, allowed themselves to become isolated from the other left-wing parties and were eventually driven underground when Gonzalez Videla brought in his anti-Communist law in 1948. These events were in no sense a precedent for what was to happen after 1970, when it would be the turn of the middle-class partners in Allende's alliance to be weakened and 'colonised' by the Marxist groups.

In 1935, the Comintern had recommended alliances with 'bourgeois democratic parties' and the advantages of this strategy were defined by the General Secretary, Dimitrov, in words that have a very contemporary ring:

The formation of a joint People's Front providing for joint

action with Social Democratic parties is a necessity. Cannot we endeavour to unite the Communist, Social Democratic, Catholic and other workers? Comrades, you will remember the ancient tale of the capture of Troy. The attacking army was unable to achieve victory until, with the aid of the Trojan Horse, it penetrated to the very heart of the enemy camp. We, revolutionary workers, should not be shy of using the same tactics.[14]

The strategy of the Trojan horse was transplanted to Chile that same year in the person of a very singular Peruvian called Eudocio Ravines. Ravines was a Peruvian Comintern agent who had been sent direct from Moscow to sort out the Peruvian Communist Party, then regarded as rather backward and disorganised. The Chilean Communist leader, Elias Laferrte, denies in his memoirs that Ravines arrived as early as 1935, in the effort to take personal credit for the adoption of popular front tactics. There is evidence to suggest, however, that Ravines did indeed arrive in that year, travelling with a false passport under the name of Jorge Montero.

At any rate, there is no dispute about Ravines's personal character: not only was he resented as an arrogant outsider, but it was later discovered that his commitment to Hitler's cause after the signing of the Nazi–Soviet pact in 1939 went beyond the bounds of political expediency. He pocketed large sums of money from the German embassy in Santiago, and became one of the advocates of an 'ideological entente' between Communism and Fascism.[15] It is one of the larger ironies of Chilean history that the country's first attempt to build an 'anti-Fascist' alliance should have begun under the sponsorship of a paid Nazi agent.

Under Ravines's direction, the Chilean Communists made overtures to the Radical Party, a loose coalition of anti-clerical liberals and of middling farmers and rising businessmen that was held together by common ambition rather than principle. As one analyst puts it, 'the real basis for the construction of the popular front in Chile was merely the slightly left-of-centre Radical Party's desperate urge to obtain control of government patronage and the Communists' willingness to help them to do so'.[16] Aguirre Cerda, the candidate of the Communists, Socialists and Radicals who made up the first popular front in the 1938 presidential elections, was no fire-breathing revolutionary but a fairly conservative landowner. What finally got him into power was another of those awkward things that Chile's Marxist historians would prefer to gloss over. Aguirre Cerda would not have been elected without the support of those local Fascists that his popular front was theoretically formed to combat.

The backdrop was a comic-opera incident that took place on 5 September 1938, when the Chilean Nazi movement, led by Gonzalez von Marees, staged a clumsy imitation of the Munich beer-hall putsch by occupying the Caja de Seguros Obreros near the presidential palace. The government of Arturo Alessandri did not scruple to deal with them sternly. The building was surrounded by the police, and only one of the sixty-two Nazis inside escaped alive. There was an outcry after this massacre, and the Nazis, together with Carlos Ibanez, the former populist *caudillo* who had been planning to run in the elections, switched their support to the popular front. Their backing was probably worth between 30,000 and 40,000 votes, and Aguirre Cerda defeated his conservative opponent in the ensuing elections with a majority of only about 5,000 votes.

Chile's first popular front thus represented a strange *mariage de convenance* between Marxists, Radicals and Fascists. The Communists, following instructions from Moscow, decided not to accept posts in the Aguirre Cerda government. The Socialists were deeply divided over the question of how far they should participate, but finally sank their scruples and accepted three portfolios; the ministry of health went to the youthful Salvador Allende. It soon became clear, however, that the Radicals were not ready to undertake the programme of sweeping nationalisation that the Socialists wanted.[17] The entry of the three 'Radical millionaires' (Humberto Alvarez, Cristobal Sáenz and Victor Moller) into the cabinet in 1940 confirmed the government's swing towards the right, and the Socialists dropped out, although they returned to take office again under President Rios two years later.

Feuding within the Marxist camp was as obvious under the first popular front government as it was later to be under Allende. One of the many issues that divided Communists and Socialists was the proper attitude to adopt towards Hitler's war. The Communists, always faithful to the Moscow line, waited until 1941 to declare themselves on the side of the western democracies, while the Socialists berated them for their 'revolutionary gymnastics' and called for 'hemispheric unity' against the Fascists. Not that these Marxist polemics made much difference to the course of Chilean foreign policy during World War II, since the government did not break off relations with Berlin until 1943, and never declared war on Hitler.

The Communists had their first taste of office during the presidency of Gabriel Gonzalez Videla. The new president was regarded as a man who in some ways lived up to the name of his party, but he was inhibited by the way he came to power, since he had given secret assurances to the right-wing Liberals in order to persuade them to confirm his electoral victory in Congress. His cabinet was made up of three Radicals, three Liberals and three Communists. The Socialists stayed out, and the Communists used their new power to drive them out of key positions in the trade union apparatus. But the Socialists were soon able to take revenge for this display of comradely fraternity. By aligning themselves with the middle-class Radicals and the traditional right, the Communists isolated themselves from their former allies on the left and proved to be helpless when their new allies decided that the time had come to dispense with them. Gonzalez Videla decided after five months—in the changed climate of the Cold War—to drop the Communists from his cabinet, and in 1948 he brought in the Law for the Defence of Democracy, outlawing the party. Although this law was never applied very firmly, the Communist Party had to function in semi-clandestinity until 1957.

Despite their unpromising experience in Chile's first popular fronts, the Communists resurfaced after their period in the political wilderness as the prime architects of the left-wing alliance (FRAP) that contested the 1958 and 1964 presidential elections, and of the broader coalition that brought Allende to power in 1970. In April 1969, the Communist Secretary-General, Luis Corvalán, argued the need for a return to popular front tactics in these terms: 'In 1964, we offered the country what was in effect a Communist–Socialist government (the FRAP alliance). The truth is that the country was not then ready to give majority support to Communists and Socialists alone. It is our belief that the situation has not changed and that we therefore have to create a popular movement with a broader social and economic base.'

At the outset, the Communists had played with the idea of forming some kind of alliance with the Christian Democrats, or at least with the left wing of the party. They had backed the Frei government's experiments in agrarian reform and were on excellent terms with Christian Democratic left-wingers like Jacques Chonchol and Rafael Gumucio. They never completely gave up the hope of an entente with the Christian Democrats. After the 1969 split in the Christian Democratic Party that led to the formation of MAPU, however, the Communists turned to the Radical Party—the mainstay of the earlier popular fronts. Under the influence of left-wing leaders (notably Hugo Miranda, Carlos Morales Abarzua, and the youth leader Patricio Valdés) the Radical Party had swung towards the left after its 1965 congress.

The 1969 Radical Party convention—the crucial turning-point—may have been stacked; it did not go unnoticed that conservative leaders like the former vice-president, Pedro Enrique Alfonso, were excluded from the meeting. It was also noticed that, four days before the convention, the Com-

munist paper *El Siglo* prophesied (accurately, as it transpired) that Alberto Baltra would be chosen as the party's
presidential candidate and that he 'would be ready to step
down' in favour of another Popular Unity candidate.[18] It
was later charged that this was more than accurate prophecy
—that it was a sign that the Communists had played a key
part in organising the Radicals' convention. At the convention, the right-wing Radical leaders like Julio Durán were
expelled. They later set up the new Democratic Radical
Party. The Radicals had now set themselves on a course that
was to lead them into the Allende government—and to a
second rift in the party in 1971 that destroyed it as a major
political force.

The year 1969 was one of horse-trading between the parties
that came together in the Popular Unity alliance to decide
which would field the presidential candidate. The first party
to field its own candidate was the minuscule Popular Independent Action (API) which, supported by the equally tiny
Social Democratic Party, put forward Rafael Tarud, a resourceful and independent-minded senator, the son of Syrian
immigrants. MAPU put forward Jacques Chonchol, the
Communists named the poet Pablo Neruda. Alberto Baltra
was confirmed as the Radical candidate at the party's June
convention. The Socialists, however, were divided among
themselves—a foretaste of the feuds that erupted after
Allende took office. A powerful section of the party, led by
Carlos Altamirano, wanted to boycott the election altogether
on the grounds that the left had no chance of winning. Unlike
the Communists, who had turned back to popular front tactics in 1956—while the party was still illegal—the Socialists
had declared in their 1967 convention that 'revolutionary
violence ... represents the only way of achieving political
and economic power'.[19]

These fiery words were diluted in the report of the Socialist
plenum in June 1969, but there was no consensus on political
tactics, let alone on the choice of a presidential candidate.
When it came to picking their man for the 1970 elections,

many Socialists appeared to have decided that Salvador
Allende Gossens, a loser in three earlier presidential con-
tests, should not be given a fourth chance. A strong lobby
was formed in support of Aniceto Rodriguez, a moderate
who was then the party's secretary-general, and a much
younger man. When the question was finally put to the vote
in the Socialist Party's central committee, Allende was able
to attract only 12 votes, with 13 abstentions. He was clearly
in a minority position within his own party, and this was to
remain a serious source of weakness despite his electoral
success. Having obtained the Socialist nomination, Allende
still had to convince the other five parties within Popular
Unity to accept him in place of their own candidates. Here
again the role of the Communists was decisive. They had
named Allende as their second choice, after Neruda. After
much back-room bargaining, Chonchol, Baltra and Neruda
all agreed to step down, leaving a two-way contest between
Allende and Rafael Tarud in which the Socialist was the
predictable victor. He was hardly a charismatic figure, although he was later to display some unexpected political
talents.

The Two Tactics
The coalition that brought Allende to power was very far
from monolithic, and the profound divisions within it only
tended to deepen as time went by. As has been seen, Popular
Unity began as a loose conglomeration of six political groups,
but some of the parties within it had the consistency of
amoebas, and the tendency of amoebas to split in two and
re-form. The Radicals, in particular, managed to destroy
themselves as a major political force in the course of Allende's
first two years. The Radical Party had already split once in
1969; again after its twenty-fifth national convention in
1971, when the leadership issued a declaration in which it
was stated that 'only outside the capitalist system is there the
possibility of a solution for the working class... The Radical
Party is socialist and its struggle is devoted to building a

socialist society... We accept historical materialism and the idea of class struggle as the means of interpreting reality.'[20]

That pro-Marxist declaration was a measure of the extent to which a powerful section of the Radical Party had been 'colonised' by the Communists who now, in a sense, took their revenge for the way they had been treated by a Radical president in 1948. But by declaring themselves 'historical materialists', the Radicals lost most of their natural constituency among civil servants, white-collar workers and teachers, and also lost the brains of the party: Senator Luis Bossay and Senator Alberto Baltra broke away to form a new group, the Left Radical Party (PIR) which remained within the governing coalition for a time but eventually broke away to join the opposition confederation (CODE) that contested the March 1973 elections. Those elections confirmed the decline of the Radicals as a political force: the number of Radical deputies fell from twelve to five.

The other major change in the composition of Popular Unity involved the splintering and re-alignment of the radical Christian groups and the dissident left of the Christian Democratic Party. While the major rift in Frei's party that had been widely expected never actually took place, a new group of rebels—including eight deputies and an important section of the Christian Democratic youth movement—broke away from the party in July 1971 to form a movement called *Izquierda Cristiana* (the Christian Left). Their platform was to 'contribute to the building of social and cultural elements of Christian inspiration'.[21] The new group absorbed many of the original members of MAPU, an earlier splinter from the Christian Democratic Party that was now moving in an overtly Marxist direction. Jacques Chonchol moved over to become one of the key leaders of *Izquierda Cristiana*, together with a young publicist called Luis Maira. From its inception, the new party moved rapidly towards the extremist position of the Movement of the Revolutionary Left (MIR) which supported its candidates in the March 1973 elections. No other group in Chilean politics could rival the Catholic

radicals in their capacity to catapault almost overnight from
opposition to Allende to support for his 'reformist' tendencies,
and then to support for violent revolution.

It was the rift within the Marxist camp that proved too
fundamental. In the course of Allende's first two years, the
smaller non-Marxist parties were 'colonised' by the Communists, the Radicals who stayed on became helplessly dependent
on them for political favours in each cabinet reshuffle, while
the Catholic radicals merely reflected in their own parish
polemics the basic quarrel between the Communists and the
Socialist left and ended up taking sides with one group or the
other. It may be true in most countries that nobody hates
an old Marxist as much as a young Marxist. Certainly, the
course of events in Chile after 1970 is inexplicable without
reference to the continuing feud between the Moscow-liners
and the 'New Left'. Some observers have tried to sum up the
conflict by describing the Communists and their non-Marxist
allies as 'reformists' and the Socialist left and its friends as
'revolutionaries'. Those terms do not really apply.

It must be stressed again that the divide was purely a matter
of tactics, a divide between those who aimed to destroy the
system from within and those terrible simplifiers on the far
left who could only think in terms of a frontal confrontation.
There was also, of course, a personal aspect to this quarrel—
the difference in age, temperament and style between an
urbane Communist negotiator of humble immigrant origins
like Volodia Teitelboim and a prickly, histrionic Socialist
'aristocrat' like Carlos Altamirano; or between an old-time
union bureaucrat like Luis ('Lucho') Figueroa and a middle-
class student-turned-guerrilla like Miguel Enriquez. There
was also the deep-rooted distrust by the non-Communist left
of the Communist Party's uncritical loyalty to Moscow.

The Chilean Communist Party
Among the young Socialist Party militants, 'Pegasos' became
a favourite term of abuse for the Chilean Communists. 'Like
those Spanish trucks,' students would say, 'the Communists

are red on the outside, but yellow inside, and square.' Three things in particular distinguish the Chilean Communist Party from its Marxist rivals. First, it has some claim to be a genuine 'proletarian party'; Luis Corvalán claimed that 75 per cent of the membership were workers[22] although the proportion is probably really closer to 65 per cent. Second, like other Latin American Communist Parties, the Chilean party has always been noted for its caution and its preference for political manipulation rather than revolutionary violence. Both in the mid-1930s and the mid-1950s, the Communists became leading advocates of united front tactics and of the 'peaceful way' (via pacifica) to socialism.[23] They were prepared to join forces with very curious allies, to the point where it sometimes seemed that they found it easier to do business with their class enemies on the right than with their rival comrades on the left.

Finally, the Chilean Communist Party has been, since its inception, an uncritical instrument of Soviet foreign policy. None of the great issues that have divided the Communist world have shaken the obedience of the Chilean leadership to the current Moscow line—not even the Russian invasion of Czechoslovakia in 1968. Even the Communists' tactics in Chile's internal power-struggle followed guidelines determined in Moscow. Perhaps this degree of ideological dependence reflected the provincial character of the Chilean party and its lack of original theorists.

The roots of the Chilean Communist Party lie in the nitrate fields of the north and the coal mines around Concepción, areas where there is a long tradition of labour militancy stemming from the appalling conditions in which miners were herded together around the turn of the century. It was in the northern town of Iquique, where the first general strike of nitrate workers had been put down by the army in 1890, and where some 2,000 miners had been machine-gunned in a schoolyard during a later strike in 1907, that the prototype of the Chilean Communist Party was founded in 1912. It called itself the Socialist Workers' Party (POS) and its

D

leader was Luis Emilio Recabarren, a former typographer. After the Bolshevik revolution, the party changed its name and applied for admission to the Third International—which was not granted until 1928, after it had been driven underground, since the Comintern leaders had doubts whether the Chilean Communists were sufficiently 'bolshevised'.

From the very beginning, the Chilean Communists stressed the importance of parliamentary tactics, although some of their early recruits were drawn from anarchist groups. Recabarren was elected as a deputy for Antofagasta as early as 1921. But throughout the party's history, there was a continuing struggle between those who wanted to work within the parliamentary system and those who believed it could be overthrown by violence or a general strike. The ultras criticised the leadership, for example, for failing to take advantage of the revolt of the naval garrisons in Coquimbo and Talcahuano in 1931[24] although one former Communist has recently revealed that Galo Gonzalez, later to become the party's secretary-general, advised the rebels to shoot their officers so that there would be 'no turning back'.[25] In the early 1930s the extremists did succeed—temporarily—in dictating party policy: the result was a declaration that the Soviet Union was the only country recognised by the Communists and a madcap assault on an army barracks in Copiapo in 1933.

But apart from this brief interlude (in which the Comintern, of course, was advocating 'direct action' and armed struggle) the Chilean Communists rejected the temptation of violent tactics. In a series of internal debates after World War II, the extremists were silenced or expelled. After the party was outlawed for the second time under President Gabriel Gonzalez Videla's 'Law for the Defence of Democracy' (1948), a group of young Turks planned to resort to guerrilla tactics. They were expelled. Those, like Clotario Blest, then the Communist president of the trade union federation, who came back from Havana after the Cuban revolution advocating Castroite tactics at home were also driven out.

Even while the party was still outlawed, at its tenth conference in 1956 it was reaffirmed that the road to power lay through popular front tactics. In 1962, Luis Corvalán, the party's secretary-general since 1958, was writing that 'at this stage of the development of events in Chile it may be affirmed that objectively, the revolutionary process is taking a peaceful road, the road that, in accordance with reality, our Party pointed out'.[26] Unlike the Socialist Party, which has always been a congeries of warring factions, the Communist Party has been able to impose the current line on all its members, or has been ready to purge the recalcitrants. Its internal discipline is unequalled by any other Chilean political group. It is illustrated by the tight control over the parliamentary deputation that is exercised by the leadership; a leading ex-Communist reports that (in accordance with standard Communist practice) 60 per cent of his salary was taken by the party as a contribution to its finances when he was serving as a deputy.[27]

Despite the façade, the Chilean Communist Party is not entirely monolithic. The stand taken by Secretary-General Corvalán over the Soviet invasion of Czechoslovakia lost him considerable support, especially among the party's youth movement. Manuel Cantero, a good orator and a former secretary-general of the Communist Youth, came to the fore in 1968 at the lead of those who questioned the leadership's stand on Czechoslovakia.[28]

The central committee includes some cultured and socially mobile men. Senator Volodia Teitelboim, the chief party theorist, has written an opera on the life of Recabarren, is fluent in many European languages, and used his flair for diplomacy to good effect during the visit of the Queen of England as well as in Havana during the stormy period in the mid-1960s when the Cuban and Chilean Communists were strongly opposed on tactics. Together with Luis Figueroa, the Communist trade union boss, Volodia later established a cordial personal relationship with General Prats and became one of the party's chief intermediaries with the armed forces.

One of the party's prize acquisitions in the literary world, of course, was the poet Pablo Neruda, who was fielded as the Communist presidential candidate during the period of bargaining within the Popular Unity alliance before the 1970 election. He was later made ambassador to Paris. Neruda is considered by many critics to be the finest living poet in the Spanish language, but sadly his political affiliations have not notably helped his writing; one of his most recent efforts was entitled 'Incitement to Nixon-murder'.[29] Another key leader was Orlando Millas, a shrewd negotiator and a sometimes violent critic of the revolutionary left who was given the ministry of finance in 1972. He became a special target of the Marxist ultras when he attacked Castro in the mid-1960s; he became even less popular when he argued, within the Allende government, that it was necessary to restore the confidence of what was left of the private sector in order to boost production.

Despite the intellectual calibre of some of its leaders, under Corvalán's leadership, the Chilean Communist Party clung to a rigid pro-Moscow line. It was the Chilean party, for example, that was chosen to deliver a stinging attack on the Albanians on behalf of seventeen Latin American Communist parties in 1961, at the start of the Sino–Soviet quarrel. Corvalán defined the party's position on foreign policy in a public letter sent to the leader of the Socialist Party, Raúl Ampuero, in the course of one of the frequent ideological debates within the Chilean left.[30] Corvalán justified his party's policy of unconditional loyalty to the Soviet Union on the grounds that 'the world is divided into two major opposing camps, the capitalist camp and the socialist camp'. While the Nato alliance, in his view, was irredeemably bent on aggression, 'the Soviet Union, since its birth, has invariably pursued a policy of peace'.

Corvalán even claimed that Hitler's war—which had the tacit support both of Chile's popular front government and of the Communist Party in 1939—was an 'imperialist plot' to overthrow the Soviet government.

Due to conflicts among the imperialists, they were unable to unite against the Soviet Union in the Second World War, and only one part of the imperialists did so. However, as is well known, during the course of the war, and more particularly following it, the imperialists worked and have continued to work for unity in opposing the Soviet Union.[31]

This Manichean view of world conflict was far from reassuring to the other Marxist groups in Chile that took a more critical view of the mainsprings of Soviet policy. Corvalán went on to quote the report submitted to the central committee of his party in 1961, in which the Soviet Union was described as 'a centre serving as the vanguard of progressive ideas'.

Corvalán did not change tack even in 1968, when his stand on the Soviet invasion of Czechoslovakia came close to splitting the party. Corvalán's own view, as expressed in an article published in *El Siglo,* was that the countries of Eastern Europe, 'as examples to the Communist movement, have a duty to intervene in or assist any socialist country that finds itself threatened by reactionary forces'. The Brezhnev doctrine might find critics in the party headquarters in Paris or Rome, but not in Santiago. The Chilean Communist Party, after the French and Italian parties, is the most important Communist Party in the western world, and yet it lacks an intellectual tradition; it has never been shaken to its roots by internal controversy and self-criticism.

The Socialists

If the Chilean Communist Party was always a party of discipline and dogmas, the Socialist Party, in contrast, was a party of personalities. It was founded in 1933, a year after the collapse of the short-lived 'Socialist Republic' set up by an ebullient and radical-minded air force colonel who rejoiced in the name of Marmaduque Grove. 'Don Marma' became the presiding eminence of the Socialist Party in its early

years, although this would-be *caudillo* could never be counted
a Marxist, and probably never gave much serious thought to
political theory. His supporters, however, included an important group of Trotskyists (including the young Allende
himself) who gave the early party both its Marxist–Leninist
ideology and its anti-Soviet bias. Later, the Socialist Party
was to remain fairly receptive to the great 'heresies' of the
Communist world, and was strongly influenced both by
Titoism, Maoism and Castroism.

The early splits in the party stemmed from its participation in non-Marxist governments: in the popular fronts, and
later in the government of the former populist autocrat,
Carlos Ibáñez (1952–8). Collaboration with Ibáñez led to a
formal rift in the party in 1952, during which Allende, after
some initial hesitation, figured as one of the advocates of an
opposition alliance with the Communists.[32] The party was
only reunited in 1957. The main internal debates have re-
volved around the merits of an electoral strategy. For
example, Raúl Ampuero, a former secretary-general, was expelled from the party in 1967 for opposing the leadership's
strategy (based primarily on elections) and later set up the
Popular Socialist Union (USOPO) which had a limited influence in some of the miners' unions. Like 'don Marma'
before him (who was expelled in 1944) Ampuero was told
that he had been guilty of 'personalism' and *caudillismo*. He
had his reply ready: 'I succumbed to a spurious coalition of
guerrilla theosophists, career politicians and local bosses.'[33]
The members of this curious coalition had their own separate reasons for wanting to dislodge Ampuero; not only had
he argued against an alliance with middle-class parties on the
grounds that the Socialists must keep their revolutionary
purity; he had also been responsible for expelling some of
Castro's young admirers from the party in the early 1960s.

Ampuero's removal left it to the 'guerrilla theosophists'
and the 'career politicians' to fight it out among themselves.
In the same year that Ampuero was expelled, the ultras
scored a significant triumph in the resolutions resulting from

the party's Chillán conference. 'Revolutionary violence,' it
was declared, 'is inevitable and legitimate. It is the necessary
result of the repressive and violent character of the class-
state. It constitutes the only way that leads to the seizure of
political and economic power and its subsequent defence.'[34]
The faction led by Carlos Altamirano and Adonis Sepulveda
made it plain that they had no faith in an electoral victory
for the left, and were in any case opposed to the idea of
broadening the Communist–Socialist alliance (FRAP) that
had contested the previous two elections into a genuine
popular front. Although (to their great good fortune) they
were eventually overruled and Allende became the Popular
Unity candidate, the extremists rose to ascendancy within the
party shortly after he was elected.

In the La Serena congress at the end of 1970, Carlos Altamirano was elected secretary-general. Altamirano came from
one of Chile's leading families, had been educated at the élite
Liceo Alemán, and had been trained as a lawyer. But neither
his upper-class antecedents nor his parliamentary experience
(first as deputy for Valdivia after 1961; then as senator for
Santiago, after 1965) had made him a friend of Chile's system
of parliamentary democracy. After more than two years of
Popular Unity government, he confessed to a *mirista* reporter
that he regarded violent class war as 'unavoidable' and that,
unlike other groups within the ruling alliance, he had 'no
interest' in 'so-called middle classes'.[35] His main pre-
occupation over that period was to create organisations in the
working-class suburbs and the industrial areas that would
have the discipline and the preparation to seize power when
the time was ripe. In this respect, Altamirano's tactics became almost indistinguishable from those of the MIR.

At a lower level, there was a long tradition of 'double
militancy' (*doble militancia*) in the Chilean Socialist Party.
An organisation of Socialist extremists had been formed in
1966 to support Che Guevara's Bolivian expedition. One of
those who went to join Guevara as part of this 'National
Liberation Army' (ELN) was Elmo Catalán, who later be-

queathed his name to the Socialists' street brigades of militant youths. In 1969, a guerrilla training camp run by Socialist militants was discovered in Guayacan. Among the students at the camp was the son of the Socialist senator, Maria Elena Carrera, one of the spokesmen for the *altamiranista* faction. After Allende came to power, these dabblings in guerrilla warfare did not come to an end. The involvement of Socialist ultras in terrorist operations, and their relationship with the MIR, are studied in Chapter 5.

This 'double militancy' worried Allende and many leading Socialists who saw that it could badly discredit the party, and the central committee passed a resolution in mid-1972 ordering all party members who belonged to a second organisation to resign from it or leave the party. This led to a number of expulsions. Probably the professional politicians were always in a majority amongst the Socialist leadership, and it is also notable that the exercise of power had, to some extent, a moderating effect on ultras like Hernán del Canto (at one stage minister of the interior) or Rolandó Calderón (agriculture minister, November 1972–March 1973). But the tension between the 'guerrilla theosophists' and the career politicians in the Socialist Party remained unresolved until the last.

The Division of Power

Allende's first cabinet represented a careful attempt to balance the different forces in Popular Unity against each other. The distribution of power was as follows:

COMMUNIST PARTY: 3 ministries: finance (Americo Zorrilla, a former printer), public works (Pascual Barrazo, an employee of the party organ *El Siglo*) and labour (José Oyarce)

SOCIALIST PARTY: 4 ministries: the interior (José Tohá, a journalist), foreign affairs (Clodomiro Almeyda, a jurist), housing (Carlos Cortes) and minister secretary to the cabinet (Jaime Suarez, a sociologist)

RADICAL PARTY: 3 ministries: education (Mario Astorga), defence (Alejandro Rios) and mining (Orlando Cantuarias)

SOCIAL DEMOCRATIC PARTY: 2 ministries: land and colonisation (Humberto Martones) and public health (Oscar Jimenez)

API: the ministry of justice (Lisandro Cruz)

MAPU: the ministry of agriculture (Jacques Chonchol)

The key post of minister of economics went to Pedro Vuskovic, an 'independent' Marxist at that stage closely aligned with the Communist Party.

This basic division of office between the parties within Popular Unity was maintained more or less intact until the first major cabinet reshuffle in June 1972 when the Socialists gained an extra post, Carlos Matus replacing Pedro Vuskovic as economics minister. The internal stability of Allende's government depended on carefully playing off the two Marxist parties against each other. This was partly accomplished by appointing junior ministers to 'balance' ministers from a different party. Thus the Communist under-secretary for the interior, Daniel Vergara, played understudy to a whole series of Socialist ministers—and later to General Prats Gonzalez. For the whole of Allende's first two years, the Communists dominated the key economic posts from the ministry of economy itself, which was transferred from a Socialist with a very similar background and then to a MAPU militant, Fernando Flores. This was significant, because the main conflict between the Marxists and the opposition parties over Allende's first two years centred on the government's attempts to extend its grip over the private sector of the economy.

Notes to this chapter are on page 207

CHAPTER THREE

Economics Is Power

One thing that must be said for the group of Marxist economists who rose to power with Allende is that they were quite
remarkable simplifiers. They subscribed to a conspiracy
theory of economics according to which the low growth rate
of the Chilean economy (the average annual rate was only
2·7 per cent between 1967 and 1970) could be explained by
the 'monopolistic' concentration of key industries in private
hands and the 'exploitation' practised by foreign investors.
They argued that the takeover of the basic means of production by the state would put an end to Chile's chronic inflation,
to wastage in industry and the creeping process of foreign
penetration of the economy. They believed that by expropriating the 'excess profits' of private industry they could
transfer greater resources to social projects like better housing and that by confiscating foreign interests—above all the
American-owned copper corporations—they would prevent
the country's wealth from being shipped abroad. They maintained that the redistribution of wealth and income was the
only way of promoting steady economic growth, since increased consumer demand would stimulate local industry.

These ideas, of course, were far from original. They were
part of the 'structuralist' approach to the problems of development that has been popularised by bodies like the UN
Economic Commission for Latin America (ECLA). It is
significant that the majority of the members of Chile's new
class of Marxist technocrats—headed by Pedro Vuskovic,
Allende's first minister of economy, Jacques Chonchol, his

first agriculture minister, Alfonse Inostroza, who became the president of the Central Bank, and Gonzalo Martner, who took over at the state planning agency, ODEPLAN—had worked at some stage for ECLA, or the UN Food and Agriculture Organisation (FAO) or some other of the UN's technical agencies. Their common approach to economic planning reflected a common experience.[1]

Vuskovic, for example, had worked for ECLA for 20 years, from 1949 to 1969. He worked with Allende in the 1970 election campaign, and afterwards became the main architect of the government's economic strategy. Even after he fell out with the Communist Party and was forced to resign from the cabinet in June 1972, he continued to exert considerable influence from his new base at the Executive Economic Council and on the board of the state development corporation, CORFO. His successor, Carlos Matus (economy miniter from June till November 1972) was cast in the same mould. Like Vuskovic, he was originally trained as a civil engineer. He joined ECLA in 1959 and joined a technical mission that spent two years in Cuba. Jacques Chonchol had also visited Cuba as an agrarian expert on assignment from ECLA. Many other members of the 'new class' of Marxist technocrats had links with Cuba. Among the others that had worked for Castro's government were Max Nolf, who became the vice-president of the copper corporation, CODELCO, Vladimir Arellano, later the director of the budget, Alberto Martinez, who took over the state distribution agency, DIRINCO, and Jaime Barrios, who was made director of the Chilean Central Bank.

All of these men had close links with either the Communist or the Socialist Party in Chile. Vuskovic, for example, had helped the Communist economist, José Cademartori, in his campaign for a seat in the chamber of deputies. Few members of the 'new class' admitted to being members of any political party; they presented themselves to the public as independent Marxists. But there was no doubt about their political goals. The role of economic planning was in their eyes not confined

to raising production, redistributing income, or improving
the general standard of living: it was part of the process of
creating a socialist revolution. Within this perspective, they
were willing to shrug off the appalling economic consequences
of their programme, which exploded the myth that wicked
capitalism had been responsible for the country's economic
backwardness. As the food queues got longer and the shops
emptier, as inflation soared to record levels and production
slumped, it became abundantly clear that the Marxist 'new
class' could offer no solutions for the country's worsening
economic crisis. It became equally clear that their whole
economic strategy was concerned with power, not with productivity, efficiency or even with any novel experiment in
socialism.

It is worth glancing briefly at their economic record. The
Marxists promised in 1970 to end inflation. But the rate of
inflation in 1972 was more than 163 per cent, a world record.
Over the twelve months up to August 1973 the rate of inflation was 323 per cent. Those figures are comparable only,
perhaps, with what happened in Weimar Germany, or with
the state of things in Brazil on the eve of the generals' coup.
And who was to blame? Inflation under Allende was the result both of declining production—due to the reckless and
disorderly process of state takeover of private firms—and of
the government's clumsy attempts to cover its whopping
budgetary deficit by printing paper money. The money
supply increased by some 120 per cent in 1971 and by no less
than 171 per cent in 1972, according to Central Bank figures.

Allende promised to improve standards of living, and got
off to a racy start in early 1971 by granting huge wage increases to lower-paid workers. But in the course of the following year, rampant price inflation (which the government was
unable to curb with its stop-go price controls), the loss of
production in industry and agriculture, and the lack of foreign
exchange to pay for imported consumer goods, all seriously
eroded the living standards of most occupational groups. A
survey conducted in a popular chain of co-operative stores

late in 1972 showed that, out of a range of 3,000 basic household products that were normally stocked, more than 2,500
were unavailable.[2] The almost inevitable result of the persistent shortages of food and basic consumer goods was the introduction of a system of rationing in January 1973 and the
creation of a flourishing black market.

The government presented nationalisation of the means of
production, distribution and exchange as an economic
panacea, and exalted central planning above private initia-
tive. Yet the Popular Unity planners were repeatedly unable
to predict the size of the budgetary deficit or the level of inflation in a given year. Take their estimates of the budget
deficit in 1971. At a meeting of the council of the Alliance
for Progress in February 1971 the Chilean delegation, led
by Vuskovic, forecast a balance of payments deficit of $29
million. The following November, Americo Zorrilla, the
Communist finance minister, admitted that the deficit was
likely to amount to $173 million. In January 1972 it was
calculated that the real figure was closer to $385 million.[3]

Growth was clearly not the top priority of the new planners, but the government claimed that the modest industrial
boom of 1971 was clear proof that a radical programme of income redistribution was the key to faster development. The
rise in industrial production in 1971 was officially claimed to
be 10 per cent, although this figure was disputed. However,
higher industrial production in 1971 was not the result of increased investment. On the contrary, the overall rate of investment fell by 11 per cent in that year and continued to fall
in 1972.[4] That was a sign both of the lack of confidence among
private businessmen and foreign investors and of the fact
that the government was using its own resources to expand
its control over the private sector instead of creating new industry or improving existing plant. Chilean industry was only
able to keep up with increased consumer demand in 1971 by
running down the stocks that had piled up during the period
of panic and uncertainty that followed Allende's electoral victory and by using up idle productive capacity. (It was claimed

that Chilean industry was operating at only about 68 per cent of its productive capacity in 1969–70.) By eliminating the wastage, industrialists were able to satisfy consumer demand —but only temporarily. The absence of new investment meant that the industrial resources were not being created that were essential in order to maintain a steady growth rate in the following years.

Thus it is not surprising that, according to some estimates, the overall growth rate declined by more than 2 per cent in 1972, while the growth rate per capita dropped by 4·4 per cent.[5] Industrial production was virtually stagnant, while there was an alarming slump in agriculture and the construction sector.

At the same time, the government had to contend with a mounting trade deficit that rose to some $440 million in 1972. That was only partly the result of the depressed price of copper, Chile's main export commodity, on the world market. The decline in agricultural production that followed in the wake of the land redistribution programme pushed the bill for agricultural imports up to $400 million in that year. The rising import bill contributed to a serious balance of payments deficit. The shortage of foreign exchange prevented the import of spare parts and machinery essential for the expansion of industrial production. It also meant that Chile was unable to meet the bill for repayments and interest on its enormous foreign debt, which amounted to more than $3½ billion by mid-1972.

In this situation, the country became more and more dependent both on the readiness of its creditors to go on postponing the dates for debt repayments and on the willingness of foreign countries to pump in money in the form of new aid and credits. Both the Americans and the major international banks (unsurprisingly) were reluctant to extend credit lines to a government that continued to attack foreign investors, refused to pay compensation for the expropriated copper companies, and was responsible for the worst economic crisis in Chilean history. Allende, who had started out by criticising his country's economic dependence on the United States, was driven towards an even greater economic dependence on the Soviet bloc.

The Russians, at least in the early stages, were ready to spring to his support. According to the Chilean Communist Party organ, *El Siglo*, the Soviets extended credits worth $400 million to the Allende government over the period up to June 1972. But much of this took the form of project aid and tied credits for purchases of Soviet equipment, when Allende's real need was for hard-currency loans to cover current budgetary expenditure and pay for vital imports. Allende himself set off for Moscow as part of a two-week trip abroad in December 1972 hoping to secure enough new Soviet aid to tide him over the pre-election period. He received some satisfaction, but there were signs that he was disappointed by the Russians' cautious response. Having burned their fingers in Egypt and having agreed to pay for Castro's economic blunders for more than a decade, the Russians may not have been over-enthusiastic about investing a large proportion of their limited foreign exchange in Chile. They also had to consider the effects of a deeper involvement in Chile on their relations with the Americans and the east–west negotiations on trade and security.

To the ordinary Chilean, the economic crisis meant endless queues to buy meat, cigarettes and oil, empty shops and chronic shortages of basic essentials like cement, tyres, spare parts, tools and clothing fabrics. This was what generated the movement of popular protest that began with a kind of consumers' revolt, the 'march of the empty pots' (*ollas vacias*) by Santiago housewives in December 1971. Some of the less-educated may have been impressed by the government's persistent claims that the economic situation was the result of 'sabotage' by American companies and local business, but it is doubtful whether any scheme hatched by ITT or its friends could have damaged the economy as seriously as the government's own mistakes. To any orthodox economist, the statistics quoted above would appear to add up to the total failure of central planning. But some of the Marxist technocrats had a very different view of the crisis. Far from trying to correct the economic situation, some of them welcomed it.

After he became minister of the economy, for example, Carlos Matus had this to say in an extraordinary frank interview with *Der Spiegel*: 'If one goes by conventional economic criteria, we are, in effect, in a state of crisis. If, for example, the previous government had found itself in our economic situation that would have been the end of it ... But what is a crisis for others, is for us the solution.' Matus can at least take credit for his honesty. It is not hard to interpret his statement. It is obvious that a major economic crisis can provide any government with the pretext to seize more sweeping powers. Few of the world's democracies have survived a period of Weimar-style inflation without radical political changes. High inflation, and the shortages of foodstuffs, provided the Marxist parties in Chile with the pretext to impose a system of rationing that gave neighbourhood committees (or JAPs) considerable scope to supervise the daily lives of ordinary citizens. These committees, unsurprisingly, were dominated by the Communist Party. At the same time, by holding down the legal salaries of skilled workers and professional men at a time of soaring inflation, the government was able to weaken the Chilean middle-class. By holding down prices in selected industries, it was able to drive the private firms that had survived two years of Allende's government a little closer towards bankruptcy.

The final goal was not a more equal society, nor even a novel form of socialism—since the Allende government was singularly uninterested in experiments with workers' participation—but rather the concentration of political power in the hands of a narrow ruling group. In this sense, an economic policy that resulted in a series of economic disasters made political sense. By eroding 'the economic bases of the bourgeoisie' through the redistribution of wealth and the state takeover of private companies, the Marxist strategists planned to change the balance of power within Chilean society. By abusing government powers to regulate the economy, they started out on a long march through the institutions that was intended to result, not merely in a system of 'state capitalism' (based on the most antiquated Stalinist model) but in an authoritarian political system where basic freedoms—including the right to strike—would no longer exist. Perhaps not all of the curious combination of parties that made up the Popular Unity alliance shared these goals; but, willy-nilly, this was the direction in which the government's economic policy was bound to lead.

As the Matus interview suggests, the Marxist leaders made little attempt to conceal their basic purpose. 'State control,' Vuskovic declared soon after Allende took office, 'is designed to destroy the economic bases of imperialism and the ruling class by putting an end to the private ownership of the means of production.'[6] The idea was spelled out in more detail in an internal document of the Socialist Party that was brought to light early in 1972. In this 'Informe Politico'—a by-product of the self-criticism session that took place under the government's electoral reverses in January—the Socialist leaders reaffirmed their commitment to 'the highest form of socialism, Communism'. One part of the document reads:

> The bourgeois state in Chile will not serve as a basis for socialism, and it is necessary to destroy it. To build socialism, the Chilean workers should use their political domination over the middle class to seize total power and gradually expropriate all private capital. This is what is called the dictatorship of the proletariat...
>
> We understand that, in the last instance, the power of the middle class resides in its economic power...It is possible for the government [by executive action] to destroy the bases of the capitalist system of production. By creating and expanding the public sector [*Area de Propriedad Social*] at the expense of the imperialist enterprises and the monopolistic bourgeoisie, we can take their economic power away from them.[7]

E

Through the jargon (which, incidentally, shows that the Chilean Socialists employ the language as well as the tactics of Marxist–Leninism) the authors of this document show that they are following the same programme for the seizure of total power by Communist parties following 'united front' tactics that was recently enunciated by the Institute of Marxism–Leninism, the highest ideological organ of the Soviet Communist Party. In a document entitled 'The Falsifiers of the Theory of Scientific Communism', the Institute spelled out the following scenario:

> Having once acquired political power, the working class implements the liquidation of the private ownership of the means of production...Historical experience shows that this inevitably leads to the elimination of class antagonisms...As a result, under socialism there remains no ground for the existence of any opposition parties counterbalancing the Communist Party.[8]

It goes without saying that the same approach also leads to the disappearance of an independent press, since the sources of advertising dry up and the state gains control of the supply of newsprint and, eventually, of the printing presses as well. The Soviet approach has been followed to the letter by the Marxist parties in Chile, despite internal disputes over whether or not the nationalisation process should be slowed down in order to increase production.

The government always refused to define just how far the extension of state control over the private sector was intended to go. In its election manifesto, the Popular Unity coalition declared that it was concerned only to break the hold of foreign companies and local 'monopolies' and it was suggested that this might affect no more than 120 of the country's 35,000-odd commercial enterprises. By the end of Allende's first year in office, however, 190 large firms had been taken over and, by June 1972 the figure had risen to at least 270 and there were signs of an acceleration, rather than a slackening, of the process. By that stage, the government was in total command of several key sectors of the economy: banking and insurance, mining, the metal industry, textiles, the *línea blanca* (consumer durables), food canning, foreign commerce.[9]

Dr Allende had already inherited formidable powers to direct the economy from earlier governments. When he took office, the state already controlled many basic services and about 50 per cent of industrial production. The state development agency, CORFO, had played an important role in promoting new industries and strengthening existing ones. It was now turned into a giant state holding company with the power to buy a controlling interest in private firms. The powers of the Directorate of Trade and Industry (DIRINCO) to fix prices were now used to favour state corporations at the expense of private firms, which were sometimes driven to bankruptcy because their prices were frozen while the cost of labour and industrial components soared rapidly. The Central Bank already possessed wide powers to dictate lending policy and fix interest rates; now the nationalised banks were forbidden to extend credit to private companies out of favour with the government.

The most depressing feature of the tightening grip of the government over the economy was that Congress, the Contraloría or auditor-general who normally rules on the legality of the government's financial measures, and the Supreme Court all proved powerless to curb a process that all of them deemed unconstitutional. At the end of 1971, for example, two Christian Democratic senators presented a Bill that required the government to define the 'three areas' of the economy and to return all companies expropriated since 14 October to their former owners. This constitutional reform won majority support in Congress, and, in the opinion of several distinguished local jurists this meant that Dr Allende should either have accepted it as binding, or called for a plebescite. The President refused to adopt either course. He chose instead to exercise his presidential veto and to call for the arbitration of a new constitutional tribunal in which his appointees were in a majority. Other attempts by Congress to check the process of nationalisation also came to nothing. When the Chamber of Deputies set up a special commission to inquire into the behaviour of state officials (or *interventores*) who had taken over the administration of private firms, the government agencies simply refused to co-operate. The commission was forced to suspend its activities at the end of July 1972.

Similarly, court orders were regularly overruled by the government. When an *interventor* was declared to have wrongfully assumed the administration of a company and ordered to restore it to its owners (as happened in the case of textile firms like Sumar and Oveja Tome) the government frequently resorted to a device known as the *decreto de insistencia* (literally, 'decree of insistence'). This is a decree signed by every member of the cabinet that can overrule a decision of the appeal court. It is supposed to be used only under the conditions of national emergency but, like other 'emergency measures', it became part of the day-to-day practices of the Allende government.

The means by which the Marxist parties managed to side-step Congress and the judiciary merit very careful study as a test-case of how those bent on overturning a democratic system can use the weapons of the system to destroy it. As the Socialist Party document quoted earlier puts it, the 'instruments of bourgeois democracy' do not allow a Marxist party to 'construct socialism'—but 'they do make it possible to destroy' the existing institutions. With the single exception of the Bill to nationalise the copper mines (passed in mid-1971) Allende did not call on Congress to pass any new laws to sanction the programme of state take-overs. Four main devices were used by the Allende government to increase its economic power through executive action: direct intervention; the purchase of shares; the *resquicios legates*, or 'legal requisitions'; and the deliberate favouritism in applying price controls that has been called 'operation asphyxiation'. The government was particularly adept at engineering labour disputes inside target-companies as a pretext for intervention. A secret committee inside DIRINCO was said to have been set up in 1971 to engineer illegal seizures of private firms. Mauro Maturana, an official in the ministry of economy with links with the MIR and its labour wing, the FTR, is said to have been specially active in this body.

(i) *Direct Intervention.* One of the most useful devices dredged out of the statute-books by Eduardo Novoa, Allende's chief legal adviser and one of the most powerful men within the regime until he made some serious blunders during the Kennecott company's campaign to get compensation for its confiscated interests in Chile, was a little-used piece of legislation dating from the 'Socialist Republic' of 1932. This law (decree-law 520) provides for 'the intervention of the central power in all industries producing basic necessities which infringe on laws of functioning freely established by the administrative authorities'. It was used by the government to justify the appointment of a state *interventor* to take over the running of private companies on the flimsiest of pretexts.

One favourite tactic was to claim that a particular company had failed to maintain production—frequently because of prolonged labour disputes fomented by Popular Unity cells or by the MIR and its labour front, the *Frente de Trabajadores Revolucionarios* (FTR). Then a government inspector would be sent in to present the management with a list of impossible demands. He might (as happened in the case of MADEMSA, a company making domestic appliances) demand to be shown up-to-date records of all business transactions within twenty-four hours. If the company management failed to meet his demands, he could then obtain an order for the firm to be 'requisitioned'. If the proprietors resisted state take-over by taking their appeal to court, the government could still have the last word by producing a 'decree of insistence'.

The case of the Yarur textile company provides a fairly typical example of how this technique worked out in practice. A government *interventor* was sent in at the end of April 1971. He promptly set out to prove that the management had been incompetent, but the evidence he came up with was, to say the least, pretty flimsy. The inspector claimed, for example, that the Yarur factory had failed to deliver a consignment of cheap fabric ordered by the hospital of the Catholic University on time. The courts therefore ruled that the enterprise should be returned to its owners. The battle then moved to the factory floor, and left-wing cells organised a series of demonstrations and work stoppages that disrupted production and finally persuaded the courts to reverse their decision. In the case of another group of textile firms (notably Sumar) an order from the Contraloría to restore the companies to their proprietors was followed by the setting-up of 'revolutionary militias' by the Communist Party and the MIR within the factories. This time, however, the judges refused to be intimidated, and the government resorted to a *decreto de insistencia*.

(ii) *The Purchase of Shares*. The Allende government turned the state development corporation, CORFO, into a giant holding company and used public monies (that should have been spent on new investment) to buy a controlling interest in private companies. It was by this means that the state takeover of most of the private banks was engineered. Dr Allende tendered his proposals for a bill providing for the nationalisation of the entire credit system late in December 1970. Although there was no likelihood that Congress would have accepted the bill, the threat of confiscation (or compulsory purchase of shares at derisory prices) was enough to panic many private shareholders into selling out. By the end of September 1971, the government was able to announce that it had acquired 57 per cent of the shares in private banks through direct negotiation with shareholders. The three major banks that were still in private hands had been placed in charge of state *interventores*. Thus, by shrewd bargaining with a hint of blackmail, the government gained control of the entire credit system, and the levers of power that go with it. It was now possible to cut off the traditional sources of election funds for the opposition parties and of short-term finance for the independent press. The political implications of state control of the credit system became obvious when the Central Bank issued instructions that no credit was to be extended to those who took part in the strike movement organised by truck-drivers and shopkeepers in October 1972.

(iii) *The Legal Requisitions.* The Allende government was also able to find legal pretexts for expropriating private firms on the grounds that they had 'failed to meet production quotas' or to 'maintain supply'. It was easy enough to create the kind of disruption that would lend some truth to charges of this kind. The cabinet issued a 'decree of insistence' on 10 April 1973 expropriating forty-one more private companies on the grounds that they failed to meet production quotas.

(iv) *Operation Asphyxiation.* As Chile lurched deeper into economic crisis and the government imposed rigid import restrictions, many private firms found themselves on the road to bankruptcy. Through widening the powers of DIRINCO, the price-fixing authority, and by setting up a network of 'committees for supply and price control' (JAP) under the close supervision of the Communist Party, the government was able to tighten the vice. DIRINCO, like most of the key economic agencies, soon found itself under Communist control. Its first director after Allende took office was Alberto Martínez, who had spent ten years working for the Central Planning Commission in Havana. During that time, he rose to the position of vice-minister for planning, the highest post held by a foreigner in Castro's government with the lone exception of Che Guevara. He was later succeeded by another party member, Patricio Palma.[10] Under the direction of these two men, DIRINCO proceeded to fix manufacturers' prices according to political criteria. Many industrialists now found themselves having to sell their products at prices that had first been established one or two years earlier, despite the hugely increased costs of labour and components. The most notorious case was that of the *Papelera,* the only private source of newsprint for the independent press, which is studied in more detail below.

Early in 1972, a special department within DIRINCO was set up to organise local committees (the JAPs) with the function of 'ensuring adequate supplies and the enforcement of price controls and fighting against speculation and monopolies'.[11] In fact, these committees were intended to serve a more sinister purpose. They really amounted to the system of 'neighbourhood tribunals' that the Popular Unity coalition had originally planned to set up, but which had been vigorously rejected by Congress—a nation-wide network of informers under the control of the Marxist parties, on the model of the *Juntas de Abastecimiento* in Cuba that were used by Castro to impose political controls at a neighbourhood level. By June 1972, 635 of these committees were said to be active in Santiago alone. By the end of the year, according to the Communist Party, some 1,500 were operating in the country as a whole.

Together with the trade union apparatus and the Popular Unity cells in individual enterprises, they provided a means of bringing pressure to bear on employers and especially on shopkeepers, who suffered from the constant fear of being charged with contravening the artificial price regulations. But the JAPs also have to be viewed in the wider context of the attempts of a Marxist government to mobilise mass support. As an internal Communist Party document put it:

> They will serve to mobilise a great number of people not engaged in political activities; to supervise small shopkeepers; to turn the problem of supply shortages into part of an ideological campaign; and to keep checks on government functionaries according to their tendencies.[12]

'The Wage of Chile'

The state takeover of the American-owned copper mines, and the effects on production, deserve special attention, since Chile depends on its copper exports for about 80 per cent of its foreign exchange earnings.[13] Some important steps towards nationalisation of the copper mines had been taken before

Allende came to power.[14] Frei's 'Chileanisation' programme was attacked by the radical left on the grounds that the government contracted to pay excessive compensation for a 51 per cent stake in Anaconda, which operated the enormous Chuquicamata open-cut mine. But the main factor in Frei's policy was a $563 million investment programme designed to double copper production in the big mines by 1972 that was to be largely financed by the American companies. Allende's sudden move to expropriate the remaining American copper interests interrupted this expansion programme. And one significant effect of Frei's 'Chileanisation' policy was that by 1970, the Chilean treasury was receiving 84 per cent of the profits of the big mines (*Gran Mineria*) in the form of taxes and dividends on shares[15]—although, to offset this, the government was also committed to pay the agreed compensation on an instalment plan.

Allende's plan to complete the nationalisation of the copper mines was fairly uncontroversial in Chile. The two oldest-established American companies, Anaconda and Kennecott, had been criticised by conservatives as well as left-wingers for making excessive profits from the country's wasting resources. (Kennecott's profits over the half-decade from 1955 to 1960, for example, had averaged 38 per cent of its capital annually.) Much of this criticism, of course, failed to take account of the spin-off effects of American investment in generating subsidiary industries and new employment and above all in providing scarce technology and managerial capacity. But it would clearly have been political suicide for any Chilean political group to have appeared in 1971 in the role of the champion of American private interests. The constitutional amendment for the nationalisation of the copper mines was passed by Congress on 11 July 1971, without a dissenting voice. This amendment contained a clause, providing for the deduction of 'excess profits' from whatever compensation to be paid to the American companies, that was to be used by Allende's lawyers with dramatic results. It was not clear when the bill was passed how Allende intended to use this clause.

The American embassy had already received indications before September 1970 that the Popular Unity planners did not intend to pay compensation to the copper companies. The role of the American ambassador, Mr Edward Korry—a highly intelligent political maverick who was later to become one of the most controversial figures in Santiago—in the months after the election was to urge all the American companies in Chile to 'keep calm' and try to come to terms with Allende quietly behind the scenes. This was a sensible approach, and it produced some dividends. Early negotiations between the new government and companies like North Indiana Brass (NIBCO) and Ralston Purina ended in mutually acceptable settlements. The case of Bethlehem Steel, placed under state intervention after a labour dispute, was more contentious, but an agreement on compensation was finally negotiated early in 1971.

The real conflict began with the discussions concerning the Cerro Corporation, a copper consortium in which Japanese interests and the Chilean government were also represented. Cerro was a comparatively new copper company·that had made a heavy investment in plant and construction; its mine in an earthquake area in the Andes was once described as a 'cathedral under rock'. Two days before Allende made his first State of the Nation speech on 21 May 1971, an agreement was patched together under the terms of which Cerro was to be paid some $56 million for its investment. The agreement was due to be signed at about 8 that night, but the signing was postponed. An hour or so later it became known that Altamirano had refused to accept the deal on the grounds that the copper nationalisation bill was about to be presented to Congress and there should be no prior settlements. When the American ambassador and a representative of OPIC called on Allende to discuss the position, he assured them that this was only a matter of 'a little trouble in our chicken coop' that would be settled in the next fortnight or so. Despite later assurances that the deal would go through, Allende apparently never found it possible to overrule Altamirano and the Socialist left on this issue—one case among many where he gave in to the wild men of his party.

This was not the end of the private negotiations on the copper companies, and the full story of what happened before the constitutional amendment was passed in July has not yet been told. According to reliable sources the American embassy came forward in June with an astonishingly generous offer described by one of those closely involved as 'the single most generous US offer since the Marshall plan'. This package was designed to reduce to a minimum the amount of compensation that the Allende government would have to pay the copper companies under a compromise arrangement. The idea was that the government would repay the expropriated companies in bonds repayable over 20–25 years, while the American government would guarantee the bonds up to the full amount of insurance taken out by the companies with OPIC or other state-sponsored organisations. Obviously, this would mean that the bonds would have an immediate value on the free market, and could be auctioned off immediately by the expropriated companies if they wanted their money at once. As Ed Korry put it to Allende, 'I'm offering you revolution in comfort and peace with the whole world.'

Allende, it is said, was at first insulted by the notion that Chilean government bonds would be regarded as worthless in themselves. But his main reasons for turning down the American offer were, first, another protest from the Socialist left and, second, a failure to grasp the economic consequences of confiscation of American copper interests. He was also counting on a McGovern victory in 1972 to alter the attitudes of the US government. And so he spurned the 'revolution in comfort' and presented the American companies with a bill for 'excess profits' totalling $774 million, more than enough to cancel out the book value of their assets.

Thus began Chile's 'copper war', which resulted in the drying-up of American credits, difficulties in re-negotiating the foreign debt, and the Kennecott corporation's private campaign in 1972 to recover some of its losses by persuading

European tribunals to impose embargoes on Chile's copper exports. By the end of 1972, there were signs that some members of Allende's government had come to see the wisdom of a tactical compromise over copper compensation. However, this proved very hard to bring about. New talks were started on the basis of a 1914 treaty between Chile and the United States that allows for a measure of international arbitration, but negotiations broke down definitively after a two-day session in Washington in March 1973, after it had become clear that a new constitutional amendment would be required to make formal compensation possible. This weas clearly politically impossible for the Allende government. Allende tried to camouflage the real reason for the breakdown of the talks by claiming—without supporting evidence—that the ITT hearings had proved that the US government had schemed to prevent him from coming to power.

The technicalities of copper nationalisation were far more involved than this brief discussion may suggest, but it is abundantly clear that not all the blame for the 'copper war' lies with the American side. Allende *was* offered an easier way out; and for his own political reasons he chose to reject it. Even more depressing is the record of the major copper companies under the new regime.

Allende described copper as 'the wage of Chile' and always argued that the main reason for the nationalisation of the American companies was that it would free greater resources for development projects and public works.[16] This failed to happen in the two years after July 1971. It is true that in 1971 and 1972, the price of copper on the world market was depressed. But when the price of copper rose sharply from an average 48.5 cents per pound in 1972 to some 66 cents per pound in the first quarter of 1973, the Chileans were not able to take advantage of a seller's market because of production difficulties. On the contrary, by March 1973, they were asking for a 40 per cent cutback in copper deliveries to Japan.[17] The poor production record of the copper mines after nationalisation, and the rising cost of production, can be attributed to the things that Allende did not take into account when he pushed out the Americans.

To begin with, nationalisation interrupted the expansion programme begun under the Frei government and left the Chileans with technical problems that they were not yet qualified to solve. Perhaps there is a lesson in this for other developing countries: that there is a tremendous danger in sending away foreign management and technicians before a society is ready to replace them. Nationalist rhetoric cannot offset the fact that world industry remains dependent on a relatively few technological centres. The Chilean managers who took over the new Exotica mine, for example, found that the problems of processing oxide ore in that area (where copper is contained in a fractured ore body that it is both difficult and expensive to process) had not yet been solved. In the case of Kennecott's El Teniente mine, they inherited the beginnings of a pioneering oxygen-injected process installed by the Americans, but found that the Chilean technicians trained in the United States to operate it had left for more secure jobs in other countries.

Apart from the inability of the new managers to take advantage of improved technology, they showed little capacity to maintain past levels of production, quite apart from meeting the goals of the expansion programme. In 1971, production fell sharply in the three biggest mines. It was down by 5 per cent in Chuquicamata, by 7½ per cent in El Salvador, and by a staggering 17 per cent in El Teniente. If two new mines (Exotica and Andina) had not been partially brought into production in that year, overall production would also have dropped. Production in the big mines (*Gran Mineria*) in 1972 rose by only about 1 per cent, compared with the planners' target of 15 per cent. The value of copper exports was down by about $100 million over the first nine months of the year —which cannot be simply ascribed to a slight drop in the world price.

Lagging copper production was basically the result of bad management and labour disputes that cannot be shrugged off (as Graham Greene, as well as less distinguished observers, has tended to shrug them off) as the result of the whims of a 'labour aristocracy'. Carlos Correa Iglesias, a former supervisor at the Chuquicamata mine, provided an insider's view of the copper problem in an illuminating series of articles in *El Mercurio*.[18]

'Chuqui', the largest open-cut copper mine in the world, rises from the desert in the northern province of Antofagasta. Formerly the property of Anaconda, after mid-1971 it was turned (in the words of Carlos Correa) 'into a centre of indoctrination for the Communist Party and a place where its slogans and doctrines would be tried out'. The former management was replaced by an Administrative Commission whose first president was a Communist, Julio Zambrano. Zambrano demanded full powers to make staff appointments during the first meeting of the new commission, and the only member to openly oppose him—Aníbal Rodriguez, the leader of the mine supervisors—was thrown out of his job and replaced by a Communist soon afterwards.

Another key figure in the new administration of the mine was Antonio Berthelon, the subdirector of industrial relations, who had joined the Chilean Communist Party at the age of fifteen and studied in East Germany and the Patrice Lumumba university in Moscow at the party's expense. According to Carlos Correa, Berthelon was 'the highest political authority in the industry, and nothing was done without his consent. He was responsible only to a Spanish Communist with an office in the presidential palace, to whom he reported daily by telephone.'

Under its new management, the Chuquicamata mine was turned into a happy hunting-ground for the extreme left. Systematically, government agents worked to winkle out managers, supervisors and technicians regarded as politically unsound. The result was the loss of scores of trained men with many years' experience. The shortage of manpower became so acute that the state copper corporation, Codelco, is said to have prepared a contract to employ Yugoslav copper techni-

cians at inflated salaries to be paid in dollars—which is a
real measure of desperation, since the terms were comparable
to those offered to American technicians under the old dis-
pensation, while the experience of Yugoslav experts in much
smaller mines where the pattern of operations is different
would not necessarily qualify them to take on the giant
'Chuqui' mine.

Under state supervision, company resources were abused
for political ends. It was alleged, for example, that the number
of company guest houses at Chuquicamata was increased from
three to eight in order to accommodate the Communist
Ramona Parra and Socialist Elmo Catalán paramilitary
brigades, which made use of company vehicles and stored
guns on the premises. 'The plan of action of these groups,'
according to Carlos Correa, 'included the destruction of vital
installations within the mine in the event of a crisis that
would make this necessary.'

Carlos Correa and other former mine supervisors paint a
sombre picture of the breakdown of discipline and standards
under the new administration. 'Ambitious programmes designed to achieve records of production for propaganda pur-
poses were applied irresponsibly with no regard for the ex-
haustion of resources, the maintenance of equipment, the repair of plant.' There was an alarming increase in the number
of industrial accidents due to lack of supervision or of technical expertise.[19]

This was not an isolated account. A similar report was
drawn up by two Christian Democrat deputies, José Monares
and Ricardo Tudala, who explored the situation of the 'El
Teniente' mine.[20] The Teniente mine, opened up in 1904 in
the province of O'Higgins, south of Santiago, is the largest
subterranean copper mine in the world, with reserves estimated at $3\frac{1}{2}$ billion tons. It was worked by the Braden Copper
Company, a subsidiary of Kennecott, until the state takeover.
The Teniente mine is something of a special case because the
American management had followed an enlightened policy
of 'Chileanisation' of staff (there were only fourteen foreigners

employed at the mine at the time of nationalisation, out of a total staff of some 7,300) and technical innovation.

After the state took over, the mine was turned over to a Socialist Party militant, Armando Arancibia, who was appointed executive vice-president with an office in Santiago. But the man who quickly emerged as the real master of the mine was Tomás Ireland, the Communist who became administrative vice-president with his office on the spot in Coya. Through his influence, Communist Party members were appointed to lesser posts in the department of industrial relations and the personnel section, as well as taking over the local union apparatus. But the Socialists were reluctant to give up the chance of staking their own claim to a chunk of *Gran Minería;* Arancibia moved his headquarters to Coya; and the end result was a bitter and time-consuming feud between the Communist and Socialist parties for control of the mine during which urgent technical decisions were often made to wait upon political ambition.

Within El Teniente, as within the Chuquicamata mine, politically neutral supervisors and technicians were singled out as class enemies: 'The campaign against the supervisors was systematic . . . All means were used, ranging from official persecution through intimidation to physical assault. All this was possible because the parties that composed the government licensed it.' Just as in the Chuqui case, the flight of skilled personnel led to an alarming increase in industrial 'accidents' including the partial destruction of refinery equipment and converters that cost $40,000 apiece to repair. The security service in the Teniente mine was enlarged and entrusted to members of the Communist and Socialist youth brigades.

The end results of the substitution of a political crusade for rational decision-making and of left-wing militants for professional men was predictable enough. Production dropped by 17.5 per cent in 1971. The cost of production (which had risen from 15 cents per pound to 29 cents over the six-year period between 1964 and 1970) soared from 29 cents per pound to 50 cents in the course of 1971. While the state earned more than $94 million from the Teniente mine in 1970 (and the Braden Corporation earned $20 million) it actually *lost* $10 million on the mine's operations in 1971. The figures speak for themselves, even if the government continued to allege 'right-wing sabotage'.

The mistakes made at Teniente were made elsewhere. When the government interested itself in a small private mining company called the Sociedad Minera Pudahuel which had begun operations in mid-1970 but run into financial difficulties, the first action of the *interventor* appointed in February 1972 was to sack five of the top management staff and to press for the resignation of a sixth.[21]

The Cost of Nationalisation

Outside the little town of Casablanca, on the road from Santiago to Valparaiso, you pass an enormous car plant which, until late in 1972, had a huge neon sign reading *'Su Ford nace aqui.'* ('Your Ford is born here.') But Fords stopped being born in Chile in 1971. The company pulled out after the government clamped unrealistically low prices on their cars, although the factory had only recently started operating. The management calculated, strange as it may seem, that it would be cheaper to pull out than to work for a single day under the new terms. Their insurance covered workers' compensation. Public opinion forced the government to do something with the modern factory it had not counted on inheriting so soon, but since the equipment is built to make Fords, all that the official planners could find to do with it was to ship in cars from Argentina to Valparaiso, truck them down to the ex-Ford factory, and fit them with new batteries and odd bits of upholstery. It is not exactly an example of the optimal use of technology.

But the Allende government's most savage attack, as this chapter has shown, was against the Chilean private sector. The political motivation of the nationalisation programme is obvious enough; so is its economic cost. The then Communist

F

finance minister, Orlando Millas, admitted late in 1972 that the losses of the state corporations in that year were likely to total around 50 billion escudos—more than $1 billion at what was then the official rate of exchange. The judgement of one intelligent and critical young Chilean economist is that 'there is no case of an important project that would allow one to say that the government managed, in any area, to increase the production of one of the basic economic sectors to any significant extent... The government set out to take over the "excess profits" of the private sector and ended by destroying them and incorporating them into the public sector in the form of a deficit.'[22] The industrialists' association, SOFOFA was driven to ask, in a public letter to the president, why the resources of the state development corporation were used to buy control of existing enterprises instead of creating new ones:

> Why isn't the money used to create new sources of work that would give guaranteed, well-paid employment to the 100,000 Chileans who will be looking for jobs for the first time in this year alone? Why isn't it used to establish new factories to manufacture the products that the people are demanding every day in greater quantities? If 1972 is to be the year of investment, as the ODEPLAN planners say, must we interpret that to mean that the state is only going to invest in buying up existing enterprises?[23]

A year later, in a major speech, the combative young president of SOFOFA, Orlando Saenz, was less interrogatory: 'This government is systematically destroying Chilean industry.'[24]

Even some of the state corporations inherited from previous governments deteriorated seriously after Allende assumed power. Driving up to the capital from Rancagua in the summer of 1972, I passed a crowded passenger train travelling at night with only half a dozen light-bulbs burning along the entire length of the carriages. Most of its passengers were hunched in darkness. The decline of the state railways under the management of Nahum Castro, a Socialist Party militant whose support for the revolutionary left earned him the nickname of 'Comandante Serapio', was one of the most notorious examples of the effects of Popular Unity supervision. It was claimed that 300 trained railway engineers were replaced by political elements in 1971, including members of the MIR and other extremist groups. Despite a 72 per cent increase in the government subsidy to the railway corporation in that year, the work of construction and repair slowed to a standstill because of shortages of materials and imported equipment. Some 40 per cent of the rolling stock was reported to be off the rails by February 1972 awaiting repair.[25]

One thing that must be conceded is that, by the way the new state managers ran the nationalised industries, the Marxists proved that they were not interested in profits. CORFO officials suggested at the start of 1972 that the losses in the 'social area' of industry might amount to $340 million.[26] By the end of the year, that figure had come to look like a gross underestimation. Orlando Millas quoted a figure three times as large. The real figure may well have been double that, but statistics are hard to come by, since under Allende, basic economic indicators have been treated like military secrets. Private companies in Chile are compelled by law to declare themselves bankrupt and close down if their losses amount to half their declared capital, but there were many cases among the nationalised industries of firms whose losses in 1972 amounted to almost their entire capital but were kept afloat by lending from the state banks.

Why were the state-run companies losing so much money, when (at least in 1972) many of them were conceded price rises much higher than those granted to the private sector? Apart from bad management, their costs rose rapidly as more workers were taken on. The El Teniente copper mine, for instance, took on 4,000 new employees in 1971, although its original staff was only 8,000 and production did not go up significantly afterwards. In the Sumar textile firm, with 2,500

employees, an extra 1,000 were hired in 1971. After the big
private brewery chain, Cervecerías Unidas, was taken over
its staff was more than doubled, although production halved
over the first six months.

It was this vast expansion of the number of employees in
state-run firms that (more than any other single factor) ex-
plains how Allende was able to cut the rate of unemployment
—although it began to climb again towards the end of 1972.
This was a political gambit, and inside the nationalised companies, the workers were frequently far from happy. Most of
the new official managers were recruited on the basis of their
political allegiance rather than their qualifications to do the
job—another reason for the losses of state-run firms and the
alarming increase in industrial accidents, especially in the
mines. There were some notorious cases of the intimidation
of workers who were not ready to toe the government line. In
the Sumar textile firm, for example, 38 workers were sacked
for demanding a system of workers' participation. Another 18
workers were sacked on similar grounds from Rayon Said,
another textile company. In Baterías Elbetia (which makes
car batteries) a state *interventor* threatened workers who asked
for a pay rise with an automatic weapon. 'You workers should
not imagine,' the Christian Democrat union leader, Manuel
Rodriguez, reports him as saying, 'that you can behave like
this to a workers' government.'

Ernesto Vogel, the left-wing Christian Democrat, elected
vice-president of the CUT in 1972, complained of other kinds
of discrimination against opposition employees. He cited the
transfer of state employees from one end of the country to the
other, away from their homes and families, on political
grounds; discrimination against the children of Christian
Democrat unionists who wish to enter the Technical University; and so on. Manuel Rodriguez, the bright young 29-year-
old Christian Democrat who won control of the Santiago section of the CUT in 1972, warned of the danger of the state
becoming the sole employer—a concentration of political and
social powers that was symbolised by the appointment of the

Communist trade union boss, Luis Figueroa, as minister of labour at the end of 1972.

It is one of the central arguments of this book that the Allende government's programme of nationalisation cannot be regarded as 'reform' in an economic sense, since it did not result in better management, higher productivity, the introduction of new technology, or imaginative new investment. The state takeovers were not reforms in a social sense either, since they did not result in any genuinely socialist experiment in workers' control. On the contrary, several cases have been cited where workers were expelled from their jobs because they had the temerity to demand a system of workers' participation instead of the highly reactionary form of state capitalism that the Communist Party insisted on imposing. Although the government signed an agreement with the trade union federation early in 1972 providing, in theory, for the inclusion of some workers in management committees, this only came after a massive campaign by the Christian Democratic Party in favour of *autogestión*, and there was a notable reluctance on the part of the new state managers to turn it into practice. The logical consequence of the continued process of state takeover of private companies was a situation in which both free choice of employment and the right to strike would be brought to an end and the Marxist parties, by acquiring a monopoly of economic power, would be in a position to assume total political power as well. In that sense, it might be argued that one of the most important lessons of the Chilean experience for the outside world is that political pluralism is conditional upon a real measure of economic pluralism.

Notes to this chapter are on page 209

Appendix to Chapter 3

Credits to Chile (November 1970–February 1972)

Short term	$m
USSR	103
Argentina	56
Italy	52
France	36
Australia	29
West Germany	28
Mexico	26
Spain	15
Canada	11
USA	32
Others	102
	490

Long term	
Brazil	10
Mexico	20
Peru and Argentina	40
	70

Investment finance from Communist countries

USSR	259
China	56
Poland	35
Bulgaria	25
Hungary	22
East Germany	20
Rumania	20
North Korea	5
Czechoslovakia	5
	447

(*Source*: EIU Quarterly Reports, *Chile* No 1,
March 1973)

CHAPTER FOUR

The Effects of the Land Reform

The Allende government's approach to land reform was one of the most controversial elements in its entire programme. The rapid expropriation of private estates (that enabled the government to claim, at the end of its first two years, that it had ended 'the age of the latifundio' in Chile) and official tolerance of illegal land-grabbing by *miristas* and Indian squatters had a tremendous social and economic cost. Land was confiscated at the expense of productivity and efficiency. The alarming shortfalls in production of key foodstuffs like wheat, potatoes and maize made it necessary to import an ever-increasing proportion of the country's food supply—a severe drain on the dwindling reserves of foreign exchange.

At the same time, the way the reform was carried out seemed to please few people apart from the bureaucrats and party protégés who were placed in charge of the new state-run farms (*centros de reforma agraria*). Landless peasants who wanted the security and status of an individual title to the land they worked were not overjoyed at having to exchange one employer for another. The anger and frustration of the middling farmers who became the main target for the MIR and the reform agencies led to violent resistance in the south, where a number of vigilante movements were formed. City-dwellers (who make up 71 per cent of Chile's population) came to discover that the government's assurances that they could count on cheap food once land was distributed 'on a rational basis' were nothing more than wishful thinking.

It became clear that on the land, as in industry, the pro-

81

cess of state takeover was meant to transfer power from one
social group to another, not to improve production. But after
two years, the reckless expropriation of land had begun to
look like one of the government's miscalculations: its own
working-class supporters in Santiago and Valparaiso (traditionally out of touch with the provinces) may not have been
very concerned about the plight of small farmers evicted from
their estates, but—like everyone else—they felt the effects of
the food shortages that finally forced the government to introduce a system of rationing in January 1973.

Agrarian reform was not the invention of the Marxist
parties.[1] In fact, at an earlier point in history, both the Communists and the Socialists had willingly acquiesced in the
decision of the Popular Front governments to freeze the situation in the countryside and forbid the formation of peasant
unions.[2] But by the time that the conservative government
of Jorge Alessandri took office in 1958, powerful pressures for
reform had built up. Chile's richest agricultural region, the
Central Valley, had always been an area of big estates, in contrast to the southern provinces, which were settled later and
more densely. While in 1955 about half of the economically
active population in the south owned land, the proportion in
the Central Valley was less than a fifth. But apart from the
brief appearance of a number of isolated left-wing agitators
in the 1920s and 1930s, there were few stirrings of peasant
revolt.

The old-style latifundio was a closed, patriarchal world in
which there were strong personal ties between the landowner
and his resident labourers, or *inquilinos*. But that world was
slowly disrupted over the second quarter of the century by
the appearance of a new class of landowners—businessmen
and mining bosses who bought land as a badge of status or a
hedge against inflation—and of a new class of labourers.
These were the *afuerinos*, wage labourers who lived not on
the property but in nearby villages and were consequently
both more independent and more vulnerable to the ups and
downs in the economy than resident workers. The *inquilinos*

themselves may have come to feel less committed to their masters as the old families began to sell out: between 1925 and 1960, some 60 per cent of the farms in the Central Valley changed hands.

But by 1962, when Alessandri's land reform bill became law, the peasants could still not be regarded as a significant political force. The Cuban revolution had frightened many Latin Americans, but it was hardly likely to be repeated in Chile, which had become an overwhelmingly urban society. It was not the fear of a peasant revolt that persuaded the right-wing parties to accept a limited agrarian reform, but rather a shrewd calculation of their electoral interests and a certain sensitivity to the appeals for reform that were issuing from the United Nations and the Americans in what was after all the honeymoon phase of the Alliance for Progress.

A serious setback for the right in the congressional elections of 1961 (in which the Christian Democrats emerged as the second largest party in Chile) frightened the Radicals in the Alessandri government. The Radicals, more than any other Chilean party, have always been a party of full-time politicians and civil servants, dependent on office and official patronage for their jobs and social status. Although at that stage many of their leaders had landed interests, they were willing to trim their sails to what they felt to be the prevailing wind rather than risk being voted out of power. The more flexible leaders of the other two parties in the cabinet, the Conservatives and the Liberals, were also shrewd enough to see a chance of heading off the pressure for a radical programme of land redistribution by issuing their own more limited reform. Their tactics were an example of a 'blotting-paper' response from an intelligent social elite to radical pressures for change that would not have been out of place in English social history.

The result was Law 15020 of 1962. It was admittedly a fairly timid piece of legislation. Alessandri's law provided for the payment of compensation to expropriated farmers at current market prices—which were to be determined by committees of local notables. The government had conceded the principle of deferred payment (farmers were to be paid in bonds maturing over 15 years, with a cash deposit) but the provision that compensation should be made at current market prices meant that there were severe financial restraints on the government's capacity to expropriate land. In any case, the Alessandri government wås in no hurry. Fewer than 1,200 families benefited from the 70,000 hectares that were redistributed on the grounds that the land had been 'abandoned' or 'badly exploited'.

The Christian Democrats *were* in a hurry. Even before the Frei government passed its own reform law in 1967, it made much more aggressive use of the powers provided by the 1962 law and of the two state agencies that Alessandri had introduced—the Agrarian Reform Corporation (CORA) and the Institute for Agricultural Development (INDAP). These two agencies became the special preserves of the left-wing of the Christian Democratic party. Rafael Moreno, still in his twenties, was made executive chief of CORA, while Jacques Chonchol, later to become Allende's agriculture minister, was placed in charge of INDAP, which was rapidly transformed from an essential technical agency into the headquarters of a powerful peasant federation. Chonchol had previously been employed by the UN Economic Commission for Latin America, which sent him to Cuba as an adviser on agrarian reform. Frei and most of his ministers did not share the radicalism of the young militants they had allowed to take over the land reform. But they may have calculated that the agrarian programme would divert the energies of their 'young Turks' and buy support for more moderate legislation, such as the bill for the 'Chileanisation' of copper.

Frei's reform law, passed in 1967, gave the government far more sweeping powers to redistribute land. Compensation for expropriated farms would now be paid in instalments according to the valuation that the farmer himself had made in his tax returns. The farmer would get only between 1 and 10 per cent as a cash deposit; the rest was to be paid over 25 years at a low interest rate—which meant that the cost to the state would steadily shrink as Chile's chronic inflation ran its course. The maximum size for an individual landholding was fixed at 80 'basic' hectares—the actual physical acreage varied according to the quality of the land, so that an individual farm might be as big at 10,000 hectares in the barren southern state of Aysén. Separate legislation made it impossible for a family to hold on to its land by chopping it up into smaller plots. But the government was prepared to recognise the right of exceptionally efficient farmers to hold bigger estates. The legal maximum for a property that fell into this category was fixed at 320 'basic' hectares, although the criteria by which the efficiency of farms was to be assessed were left suitably vague.

While Alessandri's law was aimed at abandoned and poorly cultivated land, the Frei government made the physical size of estates the overriding consideration. By so doing, the Christian Democrats were following the 'structuralist' approach to land distribution that has become fashionable among development economists. It has always been doubtful, however, whether the pattern of large-scale holdings was the main reason—or even one of the main reasons—for the stagnant agricultural production in Chile in the 1940s and 1950s. The problem must be viewed in a broader context. With its variety of soil and climate, Chile should be able to supply most of its basic agricultural needs. But Chilean farmers were the casualties of government economic policy over several decades. High inflation resulted in price-fixing, and since food is the most politically sensitive commodity, Chilean farmers found themselves being paid less than the prevailing world market prices for their products—hardly a spur to new investment on the land. Because prices for agricultural products lagged behind other consumer prices, the purchasing power of farmers and rural labourers steadily fell. This helps to explain why the average wage in the agricultural sector was less than half the average national wage when Allende took office in 1970—about 7,000 escudos, compared with a legal minimum wage of 15,876 escudos. The government was also at fault in not providing credit for modernisation; there was a glaring need for an agricultural development bank. The agrarian problem in Chile was not simply a question of how land was parcelled out. It involved the poverty of the agricultural sector as a whole.

It is to the credit of the Christian Democrats that, while pressing ahead with their programme for land redistribution, they maintained some degree of respect for what was happening to production. Indeed, it was one of the boasts of the Frei government that (despite the terrible drought in 1968 that killed off cattle stocks and halved the wheat harvest) the growth rate for agricultural production between 1965 and 1970 was double the annual average rate over the decade before it took office. It is also true that, when it came to the point, the Christian Democrats decided not to go as far as they originally promised. Frei's promise to give land to 100,000 of the country's 350,000 landless families remained unfulfilled —about 35,000 families benefited from his reforms—and the government's more cautious approach to land distribution after 1968 was one of the factors that led to Chonchol's break with the party in 1969.

All the same, by the end of its term, the Frei government had expropriated some 1,400 farms covering an area of 3,400,000 hectares. Half these estates had been taken over on the grounds that they were 'badly exploited' (*mal explotado*) —a phrase first turned into law by Alessandri that was later to prove so useful to CORA officials working under Allende's government. Much of the expropriated land was turned over to the new *asentamientos*. These were intended as transitional settlements, with a life of between two and five years, at the end of which time the peasants were supposed to decide on what basis they wanted to hold their land (the Christian Democrats themselves favoured collective landholding). The *asentamientos* were to be jointly run by CORA officials and by their own committees. The theory was that CORA would help the peasants to get started by giving them money in the form of an advance that was supposed to be paid back once the collectives started to show a profit.

In practice, many *asentados* were content to treat this advance as a salary which they could then supplement by growing a few crops and selling them for their personal gain. Chonchol later attacked the whole system in terms just as vigorous as those of private landowners or the National Society of Agriculture (SNA).[3] In justifying the later system of state farms, he declared that the *asentamientos* had encouraged idleness and exclusivity. The *asentados* (nearly always the rural workers who had formerly been resident on the expropriated farm) refused to let outsiders join the collective, and sometimes actually employed the less fortunate *afuerinos* to do the dirty work for them at derisory rates.[4] Subject to loose and distant supervision, they often settled back into a comfortable five-hour daily working routine.

Agrarian reform, it is often argued, is bound to result in temporary social disruption and loss of production—when it does not actually stem from violent revolution. The question is whether the results are worth paying for. If the Christian Democrat experiment in collective landholding failed in many cases to improve efficiency or the living conditions of the lowest-paid rural workers (the *afuerinos*) at least it did not result in major food shortages, rationing and class war. The same could not be said for Allende's land distribution programme. Not all landowners, of course, were ready to accept tamely the loss of their estates. The left-wing Christian Democrats could claim a martyr in Hernán Mery Fuenzalida, the CORA official who was killed under mysterious circumstances during the expropriation of the La Piedad farm near Longaví in Linares in April 1970. Some vigilante groups raised their heads, but they were less significant than the resistance movement formed amongst small and middling farmers after Allende took power.

Allende's land reform programme was qualitatively different from that of the Christian Democrats. It was not just a question of accelerated pace, although the figures are striking. In the two years after Allende took office, the government took over more than 3,500 farms, covering a total area of more than 5 million hectares. This meant that, by the end of 1972, some 4,900 farms had been brought within the so-called 'reformed area'. This included nearly all of the land bigger than the 80 'basic' hectares fixed as the limit for a private holding by Frei's law, as well as many smaller properties that had been confiscated on a variety of pretexts. The militants within the Socialist party and the Christian left wanted to change the 1967 law (Socialists talked of setting a limit of 20 basic hectares; *mirista* groups of an upper limit of 5 basic hectares)[5] but the government's minority position in Congress meant that it had to content itself with stretching existing legislation. The smaller landowners soon discovered that there were at least fifty legal pretexts that could be used by CORA officials to take over a farm regardless of its physical size.

The abuse of their powers by the extreme left-wingers who came to control CORA resulted in many human tragedies. The case of Sr Juan Benavente and his family was extreme only in its pathos. I visited him early in 1972, on his vineyard near Ninhue in the province of Linares. Although he has been crippled since the age of twenty, Benavente was still accustomed to getting up at 7 every morning, hoist himself on to a horse with the kind of apparatus that was probably used to get medieval knights into their saddles, and ride out to inspect the vines that produce the delicious Collipeuma wine. He had six children; and his estate covered 130 'basic' hectares. CORA ordered the seizure of his farm, not because of its physical size, but on the grounds that he had failed to place an advertisement in a local paper when he set up a family company with his aunt in 1952.

Although he was legally entitled to claim a reserve, the CORA officials offered him only a derisory 20 hectares on the top of a hill, without water, electricity—or vines. He had spent most of the past year bottling his wine (until he ran out of bottles when the state-expropriated bottling plant ran into problems) and haggling with CORA over their valuation of his land and equipment, while his estate was administered by officials. CORA offered him a ridiculously low price. Like most Chileans, Benavente was a believer in compromise. He went on bargaining, and talked of setting up a small dairy farm somewhere not too far away—which he later succeeded in doing. On his farm, meanwhile, the peasants (left without proper supervision) grew wheat for private sale among the vines and almond trees that were slowly running to seed.

It would be wrong to generalise from individual cases. Some of the worst, in any event, were the result of the land seizures, or *tomas,* staged illegally by the rural branch of the MIR—the Revolutionary Peasants' Movement (MCR) which is described in Chapter 5. There were more than 2,000 of these illegal *tomas* during Allende's first two years. Except in one or two isolated cases, the police were not permitted to go to the defence of farmers. More often, in fact, it proved that CORA and local Popular Unity officials were working in collusion with the extremists. The record of Gabriel Coll, at one stage the CORA chief in the province of Linares, is a notorious example. Coll openly supported illegal *tomas* and was one of the many CORA officials who formally expropriated farms that had been wrested away from their owners by force. After local farmers produced a lengthy dossier setting out his activities, the government was compelled to remove him. He was discovered in October 1971 in Valdivia driving an official car loaded up with firearms. That was one case among many. In March the following year, for example, two land reform officials were arrested in Yungay after the police found them using vehicles belonging to CORA and INDAP to distribute a miniature arsenal of bombs and revolvers. In April 1972, two more CORA officials were found using an official vehicle in the attempt to smuggle a cargo of ammunition in from Argentina through Villarica.[6]

Far from functioning as part of a neutral civil service,

CORA was being used by the extreme left as an instrument of class war. It was hardly surprising that farmers regarded it with as much fear and distrust as the would-be guerrillas of the MIR. Even the Chilean Communists complained of *mirista* infiltration of the agency in their internal party documents. They were in a good position to know what was going on, since David Baytelman, a Communist agronomist, became executive vice-president of CORA under the Allende government. CORA became a law unto itself. In theory, for example, the farmer was entitled to a month in which to appeal to the special agrarian reform tribunals against state takeover. But in February 1972, farmers complained that there were 16 provinces without these tribunals. Allende's legal advisers had pointed out to him that, although the law required him to appoint these tribunals, he was not compelled to do so within any set time period. While he delayed, CORA's power to expropriate small farms was virtually untramelled.

For some liberal outsiders who imagine that the Chile that Allende inherited was a backward society in which 'the corrupt oligarchs' sat on the backs of the peasants like so many Old Men of the Sea, these facts will not appear particularly shocking. But the Allende government's approach to land reform was neither primarily designed nor very likely to promote a greater degree of social justice in Chile. It was not even particularly welcome to landless labourers who had hoped to be given their own plots of land. On 1 September 1971, thousands of peasants marched to Santiago to protest against the new system of state-run farms, and were set upon by Popular Unity sympathisers. Some groups of marchers were forcibly prevented from reaching the capital by Carabineros acting on the orders of provincial governors. So much for the government's claim to represent the wishes of the peasants. Later, there were cases in Linares of peasants who were expelled from the farms they had always worked in order to create 'jobs for the boys'—rural labourers organised in left-wing syndicates brought in from outside.

The philosophy behind the Popular Unity agrarian programme has been sketched out very clearly by Jacques Chonchol—who was also one of the key figures under the Frei government. Chonchol was Allende's agriculture minister until November 1972, when his party, the *Izquierda Cristiana* decided to resign from the cabinet in protest at the inclusion of the military. His successor was Rolandó Calderón, a young peasant organiser on the extreme left of the Socialist Party. Chonchol has written that 'in an underdeveloped society, with limited resources—whether in a revolutionary situation or a non-revolutionary situation where people are trying to bring about basic changes—it is a political error to aim for social improvement and economic growth at the same time'.[7] This meant that production (ie feeding the urban population) had to take second place to the government's obsessive concern with the pattern of ownership. Two things stand out in Chonchol's analysis of agrarian reform. The first is his addiction to brute statistics—the *number* of farms taken over seems to count for more than production levels, efficiency, or the plight of individual farmers. Under Chonchol's direction, CORA expropriations were rammed through without any regard for the track record of individual farmers. Prize farms like the Mithalerecht family estate (*Fundo Santo Julio*) in Cautín or the Schleier family's timber estate (exempt from expropriation according to the letter of the Frei law) were swept into the state sector. One outstanding case involved the property of the Prieto Letelier family in Llay-Llay. This was singled out by Rafael Moreno and Chonchol during the congressional debate on Frei's reform bill as a farm that would be regarded as exempt from expropriation because of its exceptional efficiency. CORA took it over in 1971 notwithstanding.

Second, Chonchol expressed a doctrinaire contempt for the very idea of private property. Before Allende's electoral victory, he attacked the 'excessive respect for property rights' displayed by the Alessandri and Frei governments. The new system of state *centros* reflected his elitist mistrust of what he

G

had once described as the peasant's 'selfishness' and 'resistance to change' and his attacks on the system of *asentamientos*. But the attempt to replace private employers by centralised state farms aroused as much resistance as had similar programmes in Cuba and North Vietnam.

One does not have to go to opposition sources to find a stinging critique of these new state *centros*. At a special meeting of the agrarian committee of the Communist Party in August 1972, the party's secretary-general, Luis Corvalán, attacked the lack of incentives for work, the bureaucratic inefficiency and the thefts and petty corruption on the state farms. 'There are far too many cases,' he complained, 'where the peasants are selling part of their produce at the back door, and not entering it in the official accounts... Alcoholism and absenteeism are steadily growing... Neither the *asentamientos* set up by the Christian Democrats, nor the *centros de reforma agararia* created by the present government have fully satisfied the peasants, nor do they constitute the best form of organisation for the reformed area.' With a curious nostalgia, Corvalán drew the attention of his listeners to the superior organisation of the private *latifundios*, which, 'with all their faults, possessed a centralised administration and real qualities of management'.[8]

These words, coming from a Communist leader, made a nonsense of the government's later claims—echoed by its foreign apologists—that food shortages in Chile resulted from the fact that people were eating better and that therefore demand had outpaced supply. It is important to note that, under the Allende government, internal consumption rose at a much slower rate than the bill for food imported from abroad—which suggests that sluggish or declining production counted for more than the growth in demand. The government's income redistribution policies may have encouraged working-class families to eat better, but over Allende's last year, key commodities like meat and dairy products were virtually unavailable. According to official figures, overall internal consumption rose by some 13 per cent in 1971 and by 12 per cent in 1972. Consumption of some foodstuffs actually *fell* over the same period. Thus meat consumption dropped by 10 per cent in 1971 and by a further 13 per cent in 1972. It is instructive to compare these statistics with the rising bill for food imports:

CHILE'S AGRICULTURAL IMPORTS

| 1969 | $193m | 1971 | $295m |
| 1970 | $217m | 1972 | $400m[9] |

Projections for 1973 ranged as high as $650 million. It will be seen that while internal consumption rose by some 25 per cent over Allende's first two years, the bill for food imports doubled over the same period and rose even more sharply in 1973. This makes it impossible to argue that food shortages resulted from the fact that the working class was eating better. On the contrary, the country's trade deficit rose alarmingly as the government tried to compensate for the disastrous effects of a policy of hasty expropriation of private farms by buying food abroad. The share of imports in Chile's total food supply was only 19 per cent in 1970. Two years later, the proportion had nearly doubled—to 35 per cent—and was expected to rise again in 1973, when Rolandó Calderón, then the agriculture minister, estimated that the country would be spending at least $480 million on imported foodstuffs. When Allende was overthrown, the country had sufficient grain left for its needs for about four days only.

A series of recent reports on Chilean agriculture confirm the impression that food production suffered as a result of land redistribution. A recent report by a team of economists at the University of Chile[10] took issue with official production figures, and suggested that overall food production may have fallen by as much as 12 per cent between 1970 and 1972 and was likely to fall by a further 10 per cent in 1973. For some key products, the decline was much sharper. Internal production of beef, for example, was estimated to have fallen by 60 per cent over Allende's first two years—partly the result of the early decimation of stocks by farmers who feared imminent expropriation. Estimated wheat production in 1972 was only about 700,000 tons, compared with 1.36 million tons the previous year. That led to dependence on foreign sources for more than half of the country's wheat; wheat imports rose from some 400,000 tons in 1970 to 750,000 tons in 1972, placing a severe strain on the country's limited port facilities.[11] Production of maize and rice also fell—despite the fact that the cultivated area actually increased slightly between 1971 and 1972.

The reasons for the decline in production (which was not attributable to the vagaries of the climate) are not difficult to locate. They included the lack of confidence of private farmers, who could hardly be expected to invest much in their properties while they feared government-directed or illegal expropriation; the government's totally unrealistic system of controlled prices, which meant, for instance, that the official price for a kilo of beef was less than a third the black market price at the end of 1972, which was bound to encourage backdoor sales and smuggling over the Argentine border; and the lack of supervision and technical guidance within the grossly misnamed 'reformed area'. A report by the economics department of the Catholic University at the end of 1972 concluded that only a third of the state-run farms had any 'system of organisation for production'.

At the same time, state farms and agricultural corporations could count on the blatant favouritism of other government agencies, whether or not they proved themselves capable of delivering the goods. To take one case among many: ENAVI, the government agency responsible for poultry farming, is estimated to have lost around 1 million escudos in 1972. In July that year, private poultry farmers delivered some 2.3 million chickens to the market, while ENAVI delivered 740,000. Three months later, in September, the private farmers delivered some 2.2 million chickens, while ENAVI's contribution fell to 366,000.[12] Maybe it would be wrong to read too much into two isolated sets of monthly figures, but 'seasonal factors' cannot explain why state production of poultry dropped by about half over three months, while private production remained more or less constant. One has to fall back on the assumption that either the state managers were grossly inefficient, or there was a massive and illegal diversion of ENAVI's produce on to the black market. Despite its poor record, ENAVI was given privileged access to the government-controlled supply of important feedstuffs like vegetable oils, fishmeal and imported grain.

The government also argued, in an attempt at self-justification, that the food shortages were partly due to the sinister intrigues of black-market racketeers. Allende proposed Cuban-style penalties for 'economic crimes' early in 1973. By that stage, there were said to be some 30,000 people more or less fully engaged in black-market activities. But it was clear that the main fault for this situation lay in the government's attempt to impose unrealistic prices on farmers and shopkeepers in conditions of general scarcity. Since the government distribution agency, DINAC, was handling most of Chile's food products at the end of 1972 (and only a single private distribution agency, CODINA, had survived the nationalisation programme) it was very hard to see how so many goods were reaching the black market without the complicity of a large number of government employees. But when a small chicken fetches five times its official price on the black market, who can be surprised that a lot of people are in on the racket? The solution lay, not in officially-sponsored conspiracy theories, but in more efficient production and a new respect for market forces.

The idea of land reform, in liberal-minded circles, is un-controversial. There is every reason to believe that a fair distribution of land in any developing society will help to remove one of the most potent reasons for social conflict and peasant revolt—a lesson that was learned the hard way in Vietnam. For historical reasons (and notably the fact that the original Spanish settlers, finding the Central Valley sparsely populated, decided to carve it up into big estates rather than apply the *encomienda* system of smaller grants designed to harness Indian labour that was tried out in other colonies) Chile was until recently one of the Latin-American countries where the contrast between the big landowner and the wage labourer seemed most extreme. As late as 1965, it was estimated that 1.3 per cent of the farmers, on estates bigger than 1,000 hectares, owned nearly three-quarters of the cultivated land. Frei's reforms changed that pattern radically. And under Chonchol's direction a totally new pattern emerged, verging on state monopoly of commercial farming. It was estimated that, by the end of 1972, nearly three-quarters of the cultivated land had been brought within the 'reformed area'.

This transformation was accomplished without much bloodshed—fewer than twenty people died in the countryside in clashes concerning the land reform programme during Allende's first two years. But an atmosphere of class hatred was built up, and, as the *miristas* and the extremists within the government coalition turned confiscated farms into guerrilla bases and the farmers, in turn, organised self-defence groups, the scene was set for an eventual violent confrontation. The structuralist argument that redistribution of land would provide more and cheaper food for the urban working-class proved to be as much of a sham as the government's early promise to end inflation. The decline in production and the consequent food shortages made rationing inevitable. Santiago became a city of constant queues, and of blatant black marketeering in the side streets. The government's total disregard for market forces—demonstrated by unrealistic price controls—and for incentives for individual producers was the major reason for the chaos in the countryside. This analysis was confirmed by an interesting document prepared by ODEPA, one of the technical agencies subordinate to the ministry of agriculture, in February 1973. The ODEPA planners pointed out that the agrarian reform did not appeal to the peasants because:

Instead of leaving them free to develop as they wish, they

are forced to work within a Marxist system that is remote from their experience. They are fighting to own their own land . . . But, contrary to what they want, they are being brought within a new system in which they are merely state workers, subordinate to state functionaries... And so an enormous bureaucracy is being formed, where what is happening is what inevitably happens when a bureaucracy reaches this unwieldy size: it is impossible to administer things efficiently.[13]

Chile has become a text-book example of the folly of applying a doctrinaire conception of land reform without regard for local conditions or public reactions. The doubts and criticisms of the government's own planners made a nonsense of the bland talk of 'the social cost of building socialism' that found echo in the writings of Allende's apologists abroad, and explain why agricultural production was officially expected to drop by more than 20 per cent in 1973.[14]

Notes to this chapter are on page 210

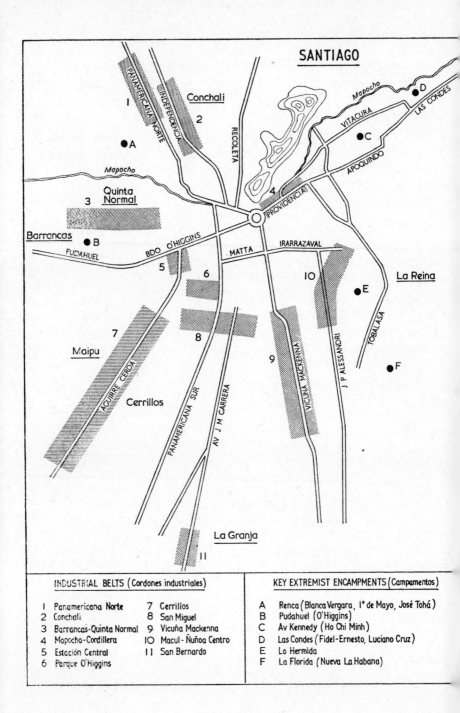

SANTIAGO

INDUSTRIAL BELTS (Cordones industriales)

1 Panamericana Norte
2 Conchali
3 Barrancas-Quinta Normal
4 Mapocho-Cordillera
5 Estación Central
6 Parque O'Higgins

7 Cerrillos
8 San Miguel
9 Vicuña Mackenna
10 Macul - Ñuñoa Centro
11 San Bernardo

KEY EXTREMIST ENCAMPMENTS (Campamentos)

A Renca (Blanca Vergara, 1º de Mayo, José Tohá)
B Pudahuel (O'Higgins)
C Av Kennedy (Ho Chi Minh)
D Las Condes (Fidel-Ernesto, Luciano Cruz)
E Lo Hermida
F La Florida (Nueva La Habana)

CHAPTER FIVE

The Ultras

The Threat to Santiago
During a dispute with his military ministers in January 1973, Allende is said to have exclaimed that, if they abandoned him and a civil war situation developed in Chile, he would not take refuge in Cuba. 'I will take refuge in the *Cordón de Cerillos*, and you will never get me out.'[1] The Cordón de Cerillos is one of Santiago's main industrial belts, running along the road leading out to the old Cerillos airport, from which it takes its name. The workers in this area gained a reputation for militancy in June 1972, when they formed an organisation to press for the state takeover of private firms, including the Perlak canning company, the Polycron textile business, and an important aluminium company. Later, during the October strikes, the workers of the Cordón de Cerillos took part in a wave of illegal seizures of businesses whose proprietors or employees had stopped work. The new workers' organisation in the Cordón de Cerillos, dominated by Socialist left-wingers and the Movement of the Revolutionary Left, was the prototype for similar militant groupings in the other major industrial belts: in Vicuña Mackenna, Panamericana Norte, San Miguel, Barrancas and Mapocho (see map). These movements of the *cordones* eventually took the name of Communal Commandos.

Allende's outburst to the military may have been an empty threat, but not because the workers in state-run industries in the *cordones* lack militancy or organisation. Allende's problem was that the *cordones* were less his territory, than the territory of revolutionary ultras. He made the gesture, some days after his conversation with the military, of setting up office temporarily in an expropriated textile firm, Sumar, in the Cordón de Cerillos, where he passed the time talking to the workers about (amongst other things) the perils of alcoholism in Chile.[2] But the gesture of Carlos Altamirano a few days later was rather more effective. At his instigation, workers set up barricades in the Cordon Vicuña Mackenna in protest against proposals from the Communist minister of economy, to return illegally occupied industries to their owners.

The *cordones* were central to the strategy of the MIR and the Socialist left. They pointed like long knives towards the heart of Santiago. Together with the revolutionary encampments (*campamentos*) set up by the MIR and the Socialists around the city outskirts and along the valley of the River Mapocho, they encircled and threatened the administrative centre and the affluent *barrio alto*. They contained the key industries and nearly all the important targets for a group that intended to paralyse the city's vital services: light, power, gas, water, etc. Within the *cordones*, the ultras worked to construct their own power-base, independent from the official trade union federation (CUT) and from direct government control. They found willing allies among the militant Socialists and *miristas* appointed as *interventores* in the state-run industries; paramilitary groups were organised in key service industries like gas (ENADI), electricity (ENDESA and CHILECTRA), posts and telegraphs (*Compania de Teléfonos, Correos y Telégrafos*) and public water supply (*Dirección de Agua Potable*). They were linked together by telex and two-way radio.

In some state-run companies, particularly in the construction industry, these paramilitary groups formed veritable militias, capable of turning out in disciplined columns to attack opposition demonstrators or to take part in the seizure of factories and vacant lots. The state construction firm, CORMU, set up a special department with the suitable title of 'Department of Direct Action' (*Departamento de Ejecución*

Directa) that was responsible for co-ordinating operations of this kind. Five officials from this company were arrested after two young Christian Democrats were killed resisting a land-snatching operation in La Reina in March 1973.[3]

As these examples suggest, the new breed of state managers were concerned with more than the battle for production. There was clearly a great deal that a sympathetic *interventor* could do to help the MIR and the Socialist extremists: he could provide company cars and equipment (the 'hard hats' in use on construction sites were always handy in a demonstration) and company time for 'political education' sessions and demonstrations, and company machinery to make light arms.

Military intelligence received reports early in 1973 that foreign military instructors—including Cubans, Czechs and East Germans—had been allowed access to state-run industries in the Cordón de Cerillos, and that large quantities of arms (especially of Czechoslovakian origin) had been stockpiled. There were also reports that two metal companies had been producing simple bazookas at the request of the MIR. Samples of the rubber-truncheons, Korean-style batons (two sticks tied together at one end with a piece of leather) and gas masks produced in state-run firms could be viewed at any left-wing political rally in Santiago by the end of 1972. But the true extent of these preparations in the *cordones* astounded the officers who uncovered huge arms caches after the coup. The number of foreign instructors was found to be more than 2,000 which partly explained why the government had refused to release statistics on foreign immigration for the past two years.

Within the *cordones*, and the workers' suburbs of Santiago, the MIR were able to make virtually unimpeded progress towards creating a situation of 'dual power'—or, as they preferred to describe it, of 'popular power'. By February 1973, a rudimentary central committee of the Communal Commandos had sprung into existence that took the lead (with Altamirano and the Socialist left) in attacking the 'Millas project' to define the public sector of the economy. At that stage,

representatives of the Communal Commandos in the major
industrial belts issued a manifesto whose key demands gave
some idea of their political goals:

1. No enterprise should be handed back if there is a broad
consensus among its workers opposing that . . .
5. The [Millas] project should be withdrawn immediately
and a new project [defining the public sector] should be
prepared in consultation with the workers and the co-
ordinators of the *cordones.*
6. Enterprises should be directed and administered only
by the workers and not in co-operation with the proprietors.
7. The big private distribution companies should be
expropriated.
8. All farms bigger than 40 basic hectares should be
expropriated.
9. There must be workers' control of production and
popular control of prices and distribution . . .
12. Expropriation . . . of all industries that produce goods
of primary necessity.
13. Direct control of distribution through the 'people's
stores'.[4]

The leaders of the *cordones* took the line of the Marxist
ultras: that there must be no pause for consolidation, that
the revolution must be pushed forward. They also made it
clear that, if there were signs that Allende wished to call a
halt to the nationalisation process, they would bring direct
pressure to bear on him in the form of street demonstrations,
barricades, and illegal seizures of firms—including state-run
firms whose management they found too cautious. A spectacular example of that was the seizure of the Agencias Graham,
a state-run distributing firm, in February 1973—a move that
infuriated the armed forces for reasons that are analysed in
Chapter 7.

According to Victor Toro, the leader of the industrial wing
of the MIR, the Workers' Revolutionary Front (FTR),

> The Communal Commandos are an organisation that is independent of political parties and of the government, independent of the bourgeois state. They are an organisation of alternative power, alternative to that of the bourgeoisie, and that is why they have their own platforms and programmes . . . [5]

The key phrase is 'alternative power'. The 'independence' of the Communal Commandos was only partially real; certainly, they were not affiliated to the trade union apparatus or the existing parties, and were loosely structured—to the enormous distaste of the Communists who would have liked to have seen them transformed into a passive arm of the CUT. The MIR always laid great stress on revolutionary spontaneity. But the Communal Commandos were merely part of a broader strategy for revolution, part of a process of mass mobilisation that (or so the ultras believed) would make the process set in motion in November 1970 irreversible and create the forces that they hoped would be able to take on and defeat the armed forces in the event of a civil war and crush the opposition if it attempted a second 'national strike'. They might have managed that if the military had waited longer to intervene. The Communal Commandos, and the committees set up in the workers' suburbs were intended as the Soviets of the new Chile.

The Government and the Guevarists
The Communal Commandos sprang into existence after June 1972, but much of the groundwork had been done during the first eighteen months of the Allende government. While the 'long march through the institutions' continued, the MIR had been preparing to consummate the revolution by different means. The MIR is a potential guerrilla force with its own clearly-defined structure and organisation, including a series of 'fronts' grouping together peasants, industrial workers and *pobladores* (slum-dwellers). But it always had an ambiguous relationship with the Popular Unity government,

since it had always enjoyed close contacts with the ultras in
the Socialist Party, and more recently with the radical Catholic groups as well. The MIR staged a number of joint demonstrations with Socialists and radical Catholics, notably in the
southern city of Concepción, but also in Santiago, where a
meeting in honour of the Colombian revolutionary priest,
Camilo Torres (killed in 1966), was held in mid-February
1973.[6] It joined forces with the *Izquierda Cristiana* (headed
by Jacques Chonchol) to contest the elections in the trade
union federation in mid-1972. An internal party document
of the MIR, dated 1 November 1972, that I was shown on a
visit to Santiago early the following year, states that 'we are
working towards the creation of a co-ordinating committee
in conjunction with important sections of the Socialist Party
and the *Izquierda Cristiana*'. It was not publicly admitted
whether such a committee was formally set up, but there is
no doubt that, on an informal basis, there was close collusion
between Altamirano, the leaders of *Izquierda Cristiana*, and
the MIR. They were joined by the faction of the MAPU
headed by Oscar Garretón that was expelled from the main
body of the party after the March 1973 election.

At a local level, government support for the MIR came
from managers of state-run firms and officials of the land
reform agency, CORA. There is considerable evidence of
members of both groups serving as a channel for arms for
the MIR; the Christian Democratic senator, Rafael Moreno,
accused Socialist executives in the national airline LAN, of
conducting an illicit traffic in arms in 1972. Socialist militants were also ready, on occasion, to try out guerrilla tactics
themselves. In July 1972, military intelligence uncovered a
plot to attack the president's private residence in the Avenida
Tomas Moro. This was organised by a group calling itself
the 'July 16th Commando of the National Liberation Army'
and it included a number of Socialist Party members, notably a certain Arturo Hoffman, formerly the private secretary
of Allende's sister, the Socialist deputy Laura Allende. The
motives of the men involved in this plot remain obscure. It

may well be that they were hoping to practise 'the Reichstag fire technique' by making their attack on Allende's home appear to be the work of right-wing conspirators.[7]

Whatever the truth of the matter, the police conducted a thorough search for the plotters which led them to the Lo Hermida *población*, where a shooting incident took place and one civilian was killed. This incident created a major political furore, and the Socialists and *miristas* organised protest rallies in the capital against 'police repression'. Allende responded to the outcry from the far left by sacking the head of Investigaciones (the Chilean CID)—a Socialist Party militant called 'Coco' Paredes, who vanished to Switzerland for a while and returned to take up a plum job in Chile Films.* Allende was prepared to capitulate to the ultras, even though his personal security appeared to be at stake. The incident showed up the problem that faced Allende in any attempt to take action against the extreme left. A campaign against the MIR would have split the Socialist Party and would have meant the break-up of the Popular Unity coalition.

The MIR, on the other hand, had few friends in the Communist Party. In a long series of polemics, the Communists attacked the MIR and its Socialist allies for 'irresponsible anti-Communism' and 'adventurism'.[8] In an internal party document prepared in January 1972, the Communists attacked both the MIR and Altamirano personally for trying to promote class war in Chile instead of appreciating the need for 'bourgeois allies' and the need to splinter the opposition by appealing to the left wing of the Christian Democratic Party.

The quarrel between the MIR and the Communists took on the character of black humour following the mysterious death of the *mirista* Luciano Cruz in 1971. (He died of gas poisoning while asleep, according to the inquest, and his mistress committed suicide by gassing herself two days later.) The *miristas* wanted to hold a public wake for Cruz in the local headquarters of the trade union federation (CUT) in

---

* He was killed in the fighting after the coup.

Concepción. The Socialist secretary-general of the CUT, who was then Hernán del Canto (who later became minister of the interior) gave his approval, but the idea was vetoed by the Communists on the executive of the federation. Luis Figueroa, the national president of the CUT and the Communist deputy, kept the *miristas* waiting for five hours with Cruz's body lying in a small truck before he issued the bald statement that the national council of the federation was opposed to lending the provincial offices for the funeral. Afterwards the Communist newspaper *El Siglo* declared that 'the MIR defiled the premises of the provincial CUT'. This squabble over a dead man's body was one of the less decorous examples of the deep divide between the Moscow-line Communists and the revolutionary left in Chile.

Their rivalry resulted in a series of armed clashes, notably in Concepción, where a *mirista* student was killed in a street brawl barely a month after Allende took office and another member of the movement was killed in May 1972 when the Communist governor of the province ordered the police to break up street riots.

In a new polemic against the Communists on the eve of the March 1973 elections, the leaders of the MIR attacked them for being 'formal' and 'legalistic' and for failing to realise that 'the communist revolution can only be brought about by the masses themselves, not by the secretary of a party or by the President of the Republic through a series of decrees ... The whole secret of the proletarian revolution lies in the independent action of the masses'.[10] This position eventually led the MIR to attack Allende directly as a 'misguided reformist' in April 1973.

The Growth of the MIR

The Movement of the Revolutionary Left was founded in 1965 by a handful of young Socialist Party dissidents living in Santiago and Concepción. It succeeded a number of ephemeral revolutionary groups (notably the *Vanguardia Revolucionaria Marxista*) that flourished after the original rift in the Socialist Party in 1963, and borrowed its name from the varied collection of would-be guerrilla movements that were set up to try to apply Guevara's model for revolution in Latin America in the early 1960s. The Chilean *miristas* believed that revolution would come through the combination of a general strike with an uprising of 'popular militias' in the big towns, co-ordinated with a more protracted guerrilla campaign in the southern provinces. For the first two years, their operations were largely confined to stirring up campus demonstrations against the Peace Corps and Robert F. Kennedy's visit to Chile in 1966. Later, the organisation moved over to 'direct action'—arms thefts and bank robberies, the illegal seizure of building sites—and began to build up a nationwide apparatus.

The real change in orientation came in 1967, when a group of 'young Turks' including Luciano Cruz, Miguel Enriquez, Andres Pascal and Bautista Van Schouwen won control of the MIR and also, incidentally, of the students' federation at the University of Concepción. All of them were young middle-class intellectuals, contemptuous of parliamentary democracy and the possibility of changing the system from within. Cruz was born in 1944 and spent his childhood on the family estate of Buena Vista, just outside Concepción. After a Catholic schooling, he progressed from the Communist Youth to become a founder of the MIR and one of the main advocates of the strategy of armed struggle. 'This was the stage of the armed activities of our organisation,' Miguel Enriquez recalled, 'in almost all of them Luciano risked his life. We attacked innumerable banks in that era, seizing the money of those who had robbed the workers to put it in the service of the defence of the interests of the workers and peasants. Luciano was always present, disguised as a fireman, an army captain, a loading worker, or whatever.'[11]

Cruz and most other members of the central committee went underground in 1969, to emerge again only at the end of the following year, when Allende declared an amnesty for 'political' prisoners and some of the extremists who later

H

formed the People's Organised Vanguard (which carried out
the murder of the former Christian Democrat minister, Pérez
Zújovic, in June 1971) were freed. Paradoxically, it was the
event that should have discredited the *miristas*' strategy of
armed revolution—the victory of the left in a free election—
that helped to transform them from a marginal band of bank
robbers and romantics into a credible military and political
force.

Just after the 1970 election, the MIR issued an important
statement in which it tried to justify its strategy in the light
of Allende's victory. The *miristas* based their argument on
the old Marxist distinction between government and power.
They admitted that they were surprised by the Popular Unity
coalition's victory at the polls, but insisted that 'the momen-
tary setback for the ruling classes must not be confused with
their strategic defeat'. Allende's government was in the position of the Kerensky regime in 1917, of Azana's Popular Front
in Spain in 1936, or of the Arbenz government in Guatemala
in 1954. Whether Allende would manage to win effective
power and bring about genuine revolution would hinge on
whether or not his government had the capacity and the
desire to smash 'the capitalist state apparatus' (one of those
suitcase-phrases that appears to cover everything from the
regular armed forces to parliamentary democracy).

'Our strategy of the conquest of power through armed
struggle,' the *miristas* contended, 'is today more valid than
ever, since the confrontation has only been postponed.' They
insisted that if the Allende government was really bent on
revolution, sooner or later it would have to 'break the legal
fetters upon it' by sweeping aside Congress and the whole
judicial system. This would be bound to excite a violent reaction from the opposition and spark off a civil conflict in which
the MIR and other paramilitary groups would come into
their own. The *miristas* had no time for the idea that
Allende's reform programme could be brought about with
the help of sections of middle-class opinion. 'We do not
believe that there are sectors of the industrial agrarian bour-

geoisie with which we can form alliances; still less do we seek
to protect such sectors.' They pledged themselves to sabotage
any attempt at compromise between government and opposition, to organise 'the poorest layers of society' and 'to dis-
place the centre of decision-making from the corridors of
congress to the mobilised mass fronts'.[12]

'Chilean society,' Nelson Gutierrez declared to Allende in
a public dialogue in Concepción in May 1971, 'is polarised
into two enemy camps: on the one side, the ruling classes—
both inside and outside the country—and their political
organs, the Christian Democrat, National and Radical Democratic parties; on the other, the popular classes—workers,
peasants and the radicalised lower middle class—and their
political expressions, the revolutionary left and the traditional left.'[13] Miguel Enriquez puts it more starkly: 'The
only alternative in Chile today is socialism or fascism.'[14] The
MIR theorists saw it as the role of their organisation to prepare for the seizure of total power through armed revolution
in Chile. Their task under the Allende government was 'to
gather the forces that will bring this about. First and fore-
most, that means weakening the class enemy by hitting him in
his vital parts.'[15] This meant two things: first, the attempt to
build up a broad mass movement through front organisations
like the FTR and MCR and to acquire the arms, military
training and base areas for an armed insurrection; and second, the attempt to infiltrate the corridors of government.

Although the *miristas* regard themselves as revolutionary
Marxists, their ideology sometimes seems to shade over into
an emotionally-charged kind of populist nationalism almost
indistinguishable, for example, from 'revolutionary Peronism'
in Argentina—with the significant difference that the MIR
lacks a figurehead. There are even curious indications that
some leaders of the MIR may have been inclined to look for
a nationalist father-figure in a man like General Roberto
Viaux, more recently the hero of the extreme right. There
is certainly still a great deal to be explained about the contacts between Luciano Cruz and Viaux before Schneider's

murder. Was Luciano Cruz trying to spy on Viaux? Was he acting as an agent provocateur? Or were some of the *miristas* themselves ready, in a confused sort of way, to regard Viaux as a potential nationalist leader? The last suggestion makes a little more sense when one observes that the MIR was able to make some early converts inside the barracks—notably among the elite 'black berets', the Chilean special forces group. At the end of 1970, the army high command was compelled to insist on the retirement of a number of NCOs from that unit on political grounds. After Allende came to power, the MIR confined its relations with the armed forces to attempts to drive a wedge between conscripts and professional officers—a classic subversive technique. But some of their earlier military contacts may have helped them to prepare themselves for an armed uprising.

The clandestine literature of the MIR (which has produced an astonishing number of guerrilla manuals) provides a clue to its methods of operation. The movement was organised as a series of regional committees with an elected central committee and a delegated national executive at the top, and a network of five-man cells, or 'political-military groups' (GPM) at the base. Its *Urban Instruction Manual* is a handbook for espionage inside the civil service, the armed forces and the political parties—up to the level of the National Security Council (CONSUSENA).

The MIR has also produced training manuals covering the weapons used by the Chilean army; detailed charts showing the organisation and deployment of most regiments; and notes on the tactics of the Chilean navy in coastal operations. Apart from these exercises in 'knowing the enemy' the *miristas* prepared their own base carefully. Another secret document on 'preparing for war or repression' contained instructions for setting up secure telephone lines and postal addresses, and for establishing sanctuaries within the cities—the first essential for the urban guerrilla. The *miristas* define four kinds of safe houses: permanent hideouts, temporary shelters, houses used for making explosives, and supply depots.[16] The system seemed to work smoothly under Allende; the notorious case of the 'camioneta de Curimón' (a small truck loaned to the MIR by members of the presidential guard and used to transport weapons purloined from the army early in 1972) involved the use of at least three safe houses in Santiago.

The relative sophistication of its training manuals suggest that MIR had been able to count on expert advice on guerrilla tactics. The Cubans clearly played a vital role in supporting the organisation. Both the National Intelligence Directorate (DGI)—the KGB-supervised Cuban intelligence service—and the Cubans' 'Liberation Directorate', responsible for promoting subversion throughout Latin America, were very active in Santiago after Allende took power. Three-quarters of the diplomats at the swollen Cuban embassy in Santiago (which, with some 150 members and a large armed guard, became their biggest embassy in the world) were thought to be involved in intelligence work. Some of the embassy members, notably Luis Fernández de Oña, who married Allende's daughter, Beatriz, had been assisting Che Guevara's Bolivian expedition. Fernández de Oña often took the place of his wife at a desk in the presidential palace. Exiled Bolivian leaders—together with a multi-coloured collection of political exiles from all over Latin America—gravitated towards Santiago. Amongst this alien colony, there was no lack of Marxist revolutionaries with practical experience of subversion and urban terrorism.

The MIR also appears to have had little difficulty in acquiring arms, both from the flourishing black market in Argentina, from contacts within the new government, and perhaps also directly from the Cubans. For a period late in 1971, unmarked flights from Cuba were arriving each Saturday night at Pudahuel airport, where the planes taxied to a little-used part of the airstrip and their cargoes were transferred to trucks without passing through customs. These flights were halted after they came to the attention of the press, and it was never definitely established that arms were delivered. But reliable reports early in 1973 estab-

lished that large stockpiles of arms (mainly of Czech manu-
facture) had been built up in the *cordones,* and this may be
one of the ways in which the weapons were got through.
Police inquiries as early as the winter of 1971 had uncovered
similar arms caches on expropriated farms. The most notorious cases involved MIR bases at the Casas Viejas estate, near
Loncoche and at the Santa Delia and El Eucalyptus farms
near Parral. At these locations the authorities uncovered
rifles, revolvers and hand-grenades as well as home-made
Molotov cocktails and dynamite stolen from the mines—some
of the side-arms were probably stolen from the security forces.

The Three Fronts
While equipping itself for an eventual guerrilla campaign, the MIR worked to build up popular support through
a series of front movements: notably the Movement of Revolutionary Pobladores (MPR), a grouping of squatters and
slum-dwellers, the Revolutionary Workers' Front (FTR),
and the Movement of Revolutionary Peasants (MCR). Each
of these front movements could count on the backing of
sympathetic elements in the government and the local ad-
ministrations. The illegal seizure of houses and building
lots in Santiago by the MPR, for example, was sometimes
aided by district prefects and tolerated by the Socialist *intendente* of the city.

The MPR grew out of an assembly of slum-dwellers organised by the *mirista* leader Victor Toro, in October 1970.
At this meeting, held in the La Granja commune, Toro
declared that popular militias would be built up within each
slum settlement and would serve as 'the vanguard of the
future people's revolutionary army'.[17] In the period between
the election and Allende's accession to power, Toro helped
to organise the seizure of land by squatters, putting pressure
on the future government to redistribute city land and
recognise this experiment in 'community self-help' as an
established fact. The MIR was already starting to play the
part of the 'accelerator' of the Chilean revolution.

Toro was a particularly interesting figure among the *mirista* leaders, since he stands out as one of the few men among them with a genuine working-class background. He was once eulogised by a fellow-activist as 'a representative of the purest qualities of our working class'.[18] Born in 1943 in a miner's settlement in Coquimbo, Toro became a miner at the age of fourteen, like his father before him. Two years later, he joined the Socialist Party and was sacked from a series of labouring jobs because of his enthusiasm as a union agitator. He was finally thrown out of the Socialist Party on the eve of the 1964 election because it was feared his fiery speeches in praise of the Cuban model for revolution would tarnish the 'respectability' of the party. He later joined the MIR and was the first worker to gain a place on its central committee. He then helped to organise land seizures around Santiago in mid-1970 and to found the MIR's first *campamentos*—the 'Lenin' and '26 January' settlements.

From that time onwards, a chain of walled encampments was built up in the slum *poblaciones,* ringing the centre of Santiago. The land-grabbing operations that provided the sites for these *campamentos* became progressively more professional. In mid-1972, for example, the *miristas* succeeded in setting up a new encampment overnight in the affluent commuter suburb of Las Condes. The assault-squad arrived by night in municipal trucks loaned by the Communist district prefect, carrying prefabricated timber walls and rolls of barbed wire. By the morning, the new settlement was there, shielded by barbed wire fences, complete with flags, posters, and a sign which bore its name—'Campamento Fidel Ernesto'.

What went on inside the *campamentos?* I paid a visit in February 1972 to the 'Che Guevara' settlement in the San Pablo suburb of Santiago.

I found a collection of wooden huts laid out in a simple grid pattern on land that was originally seized by four MIR commando squads at the head of landless squatters back in August 1970. Since then, the illegal squatters had been given formal title to the land, and the state housing corporation CORMU, had provided water and electricity and was constructing a new set of high-rise flats. Another state corporation, DIRINCO, delivered food to the door.

At the beginning, there were more than 2,000 families in the settlement; but some 800 of them were weeded out for 'lack of discipline' or 'political errors'—as Compañera Natalia, the vice-president of the encampment, put it to me. Natalia, unlike most of the MIR leaders was, like Victor Toro, a genuine working-class revolutionary, a child of the slum *poblaciones*. Middle-aged, squat, and profoundly distrustful of outsiders, she had been a lifelong Socialist Party militant. She offered me water from a wine-bottle, since consumption of alcohol was disliked in the 'Che Guevara' settlement and it was illegal to sell liquor within the walls. Militants of the 'Nueva Habana' *campamento* in La Florida, also prided themselves on their 'revolutionary austerity' and meted out severe punishment to those who persisted in hard drinking.

Compañera Natalia's political philosophy was simple and unrelenting. 'Armed struggle is inevitable in this country,' she insisted. 'We are all ordinary workers here, but our goal is the liberation of the whole of Latin America.' (In fact, a large proportion of the people in the settlement are recent migrants from the countryside with jobs—of a kind—in the construction industry.) There were regular visits from revolutionaries from other parts of the continent—Cubans, Uruguayans, Bolivians and Argentinians, some of whom helped with political education in the state school that conducted its classes in a picturesque collection of wheelless buses. At a casual glance, one might have dismissed the low wooden shacks, the mangy yellow dogs and staring children as part of the landscape of any slum in any big Latin-American city. What made this settlement different was the rigid discipline, reinforced by its defensive apparatus of ramshackle wooden walls, watchtowers and guards who look at passes and ask questions.

Natalia said that she lived in constant fear of night-time raids by right-wing organisations like *Patria y Libertad*. Certainly, arson would have been simple enough if anyone had wanted to try it. While she denied that there was any military training being carried out in the camp, she admitted that commando squads were sent out frequently to help to organise land seizures in the provinces. That is one reason why it became absurd to view the Che Guevara camp and other *mirista* enclaves in the capital like the 'Pablo Neruda' and 'Nueva Habana' settlements as merely examples of community self-help with a political twist. Alejandro Villalobos ('Comandante Micky') a leader of the Nueva Habana group, publicly called for 'the strengthening of popular militias' in perparation for the civil war.[19] The *campamentos,* and the industrial *cordones,* were intended to become 'liberated zones' within the capital—and, in the first days after the coup, they briefly became just that.

Similarly, the rural branch of the MIR, the MCR, worked to construct secure guerrilla base areas in the countryside. The MCR was able to build upon the genuine grievances and the impatience of landless rural labourers and especially the Mapuche Indians of the south. It was in the southern provinces of Cautín, Malleco and Nuble that some of the *miristas'* most spectacular operations took place. Their part in staging illegal land seizures was not applauded by those officials who believed that agrarian reform required 'social discipline'. The operations of the MCR (and its Socialist and MAPU sympathisers) triggered off a serious confrontation between the extremists and the small and middling farmers of the south who saw their interests threatened and were ready to defend them if the government failed to intervene.

Cautín was a natural target for the MIR. For one thing, more than half of the country's 360,000-odd Mapuche Indians are concentrated in this single province. In Cautín and the neighbouring province of Malleco, the conflict between farmers and squatters often has strong racial overtones that are not diminished by the fact that this is the area where many of Chile's sizeable German community decided to settle. The tidy pine forests and Bavarian-style farmhouses that make

much of the south seem so curiously European are part of
the stakes in the contest for land. The MIR successfully built
upon the longstanding grievances of the Mapuches. The
Mapuches are a proud warrior race with a great mythical
tradition. Alone among the Indian peoples that resisted the
Spanish conquest, they domesticated the horse and used it
against the conquistadors. Steadily driven farther south by the
successive encroachments of the Incas, the Spaniards and the
army of the Chilean Republic, they were not finally subdued
until the War of the Pacific in 1884.

That was the prelude to the widespread confiscation of
tribal land and a wave of 'cheap sales' in which many of the
men appointed to protect the interests of the Mapuches participated as readily as property-sharks from the city. The
Mapuche population slowly declined to its present level of
around 360,000. An estimated 40,000 Indians scrape a living
on the fringes of the towns; many of the remainder are
crowded into the *reducciones,* or inalienable tribal settlements, where they farm as families and market their goods as
a collective. In Cautín, there are some 180,000 Mapuches in
a total rural population of about a quarter of a million. By
tradition a nation of wandering herdsmen, the Mapuches
still tend their sheep and cattle, grow a little wheat and some
market vegetables, and make clothes and ornaments in their
household workshops.

Their standards of living are pretty miserable by comparison with Chilean society as a whole. The mortality rate
and the level of illiteracy among the Indian population are
both about twice the national average. In 1970, three-quarters
of the Indian working population were estimated to be earn-
ing less than $100 a year, or seven escudos a day. Many of the
Mapuches still share a lingering resentment of what they
regard as the past 'theft' of tribal lands. One opinion poll
carried out by an official agricultural research organisation
six years ago suggested that nearly half of the Indians interviewed were 'aggressively hostile' to white farmers and that
another quarter of the group took a 'negative' attitude.[20]

These feelings were fertile ground for the extremists. Even before Dr Allende took office, the *miristas* had set up camp in the provinces. Many of their early land seizures were represented as *corridas de cerros* (which literally means a dash over the hills) and took the form of the partial occupation of private farms on the grounds that the owners had trespassed beyond the 'ancient' limits of the tribal lands. Often a *corrida de cerros* simply consisted of a band of Mapuches and *miristas* stealing out by night and dragging the barbed wire fences that mark the boundaries of the Indian settlements a few hundred yards forward. There were fifty-seven of these *corridas* in the single province of Cautín between September 1970 and January 1971, and the justification for them was often founded on the flimsiest evidence from the Temuco archives or the quirks of an old man's memory. Where the MIR was involved, it proceeded to encourage the creation of 'socialist communities' among the Mapuches, in which the collective exploitation of land, political education classes, and training as peasant militias were introduced.

The next step for the MIR was to organise a broader front group—the Revolutionary Peasants' Movement—and to proceed to take over whole estates and to set up guerrilla *focos* on occupied farms. In 1971, there were about 400 *tomas* in Cautín. The general pattern was for a band of 12 or 15 *miristas* to appear in the late afternoon, or the early hours of the morning, at the head of 60 or 70 Mapuches. The Mapuches (notorious for their drinking habits) were often sent into battle half drunk; later local farmers claimed that student *miristas* from Concepción had also been issuing them with drugs.

With the emergence of effective farmers' vigilante groups in Cautín, Asorno and Linares late in 1971, the main thrust of the *miristas*' operations moved a little farther north early in 1972, when there was a wave of violent *tomas* in Nuble. Here the MCR found an ally in two peasant federations— 'Isabel Riquelme' and 'Pedro Aguirre Cerda'—that grouped together some 22,000 peasants under the leadership of

Socialist Party extremists who saw it as their role to force the government to expropriate properties under the legal limit without allowing the owners to keep a reserve plot or to receive any form of compensation. This was 'land reform' with a vengeance. In the space of three months, nearly 100 farms were taken over. The Nuble *tomas* were also a good example of the role of the MIR as a detonator. The *miristas* set the pattern for the whole wave of land seizures in the province by their assault on the 'La Carrizal' estate in mid-February.

After the Nuble *tomas,* the extremists again moved farther north, and roving assault-squads swung into action in the province of Santiago itself. The local farmers' leaders later claimed that in the month of May alone the MCR and its allies had either occupied or totally paralysed work on no fewer than 147 farms in the province. The takeover of the medium-size 'Millahuin' farm near Melipilla set the pattern for these new attacks. The original *toma* was staged by militant labourers employed on the farm. The Carabineros responded to an appeal from the proprietor of the farm to evict them, and the MCR seized on this as a pretext to invade the estate with an assault-squad of about 100 peasants (some of them members of the militant local syndicate, *Campesinos al Poder,* but most of them strangers to the district). On this occasion, the owner was fortunate enough to persuade the authorities to mount an impressive police operation involving 150 men of the Carabineros' Special Services. The MCR were evicted. But most of the other farmers in the province who fell victim to later occupations were less lucky. The size or condition of their farms appeared to make no difference to the invaders. In one notorious case, a poultry farmer called Carlos Montes had his property taken away from him by force although it covered only 3 hectares. The Santiago seizures also confirmed the increasingly intimate alliance between the MIR and the ultras in the government coalition. The MAPU, for example, was behind the 'Campesinos al Poder' peasant federation that participated in many of the *tomas.*

The end result of the *miristas'* rural operations was further disruption of agrarian production, violent clashes between MCR elements and farmers' self-defence groups like the Guardia Blanca in Cautín, and the creation of revolutionary base-areas that in some cases appeared to escape the control of the authorities. If revolution comes to Chile, it will not come from the southern provinces. Santiago contains more than a third of the population, and two-thirds of the Chileans are townsmen. On the other hand, it would be very easy to cut Chile's land communications, since its twenty-five provinces, unrolling like an immensely long, narrow tapeworm down the Pacific flank of Latin America, are held together only by a single north–south highway and the railway lines that run parallel to it. Such a move would aggravate the already grave food shortages in the capital.

While Allende was in power, moreover, the *miristas* were also allowed a fairly free hand to entrench themselves in the difficult terrain of the Andean foothills and in the low brush country around Lautaro. While it was difficult to arrive at a reliable estimate of their total strength in the rural areas, there were thought to be some 1,200 MCR members active in the single province of Cautín by the beginning of 1972, and the key organiser of the land seizures in Nuble early that year—'Comandante Nelson' Ugarte—claimed that he could assemble between 5,000 and 10,000 peasants for a *toma*. The Allende government allowed the MIR to accumulate the resources for a protracted guerrilla campaign. Its beginning may have to be dated from the flight of the *mirista* leaders of Concepción into the hills after 11 September 1973.

As a result of alleged land seizures, the MIR succeeded in turning a broad swathe of territory up in the Andes along the Argentine frontier into their own Sierra Maestra—the base for a protected guerrilla camp. For more than a year, the area up around Lake Panguipulli was run as a private fief by 'Comandante Pepe', a former student of agronomy born in 1940 whose real name is José Gabriel Lliendo Vera. Pepe first emerged as a potential guerrilla leader in November

1970, when he directed the *toma* of the 'Carranco' estate near Liquiñe. This was followed by a series of land seizures in the same region, and by the end of 1971, Pepe had made himself the master of seventeen estates covering 350,000 hectares of the finest timber country in Chile.

He found friends in official quarters. He was alleged to have received some financial support from Jacques Chonchol's ministry of agriculture, although this was vigorously denied by the minister himself. He was photographed walking in procession beside the secretary-general to the government, Jaime Suarez (Socialist Party) and the Socialist deputy Laura Allende, early in 1972. No really serious attempt was made to arrest him, although three detention orders were issued against him after a crude attempt to take over the 'Niltre' farm belonging to the Bombín family in October 1971, during which some of the family servants were subjected to violence.

Of the 3,000 rural labourers employed on the farms that the MIR had occupied along the border by mid-1972, about 400 were members of the MCR and therefore directly subject to Pepe's orders. His pickets turned back army patrols at the boundaries of his 'liberated zone' as if they were representatives of a foreign power. Pepe left for Cuba in May 1972, but may have returned later that year after receiving medical treatment. In any case, there were other leaders available. The serious thing was that having been given so much time to entrench themselves up in the mountains, the *miristas* could probably not now be evicted without a major counter-guerrilla campaign.

But in the last analysis, the key to success or failure for the MIR lay in Santiago—in the political conflict within Popular Unity, and in the creation of 'soviets' within the *cordones* and the *campamentos*. The *miristas'* own labour movement, the FTR, was never a serious competitor with the established Marxist union movements, nor with the Christian Democrats, who were able to score surprisingly well in successive union elections in 1972. The FTR was strongest in the textile industry, in the coal mines around Concepción, and in the smaller construction and printing firms in Santiago and the northern towns. It tried to batten on to bread-and-butter issues like pay claims, and earned a stinging reproof from *El Siglo* for supporting a grossly inflated wage claim by the coal miners in the Lota and Schwager works in July 1971. Significantly, the FTR had an increasing influence within the media, and won control of the journalists' syndicate of the afternoon paper *Ultima Hora*. The *miristas'* attitudes to the press, however, were hardly more reassuring than those of the Communists who talked of the virtues of the 'Soviet model'. The programme of the FTR calls for the state takeover of all independent news media, and for the abolition of private advertising.[21] It is hard not to conclude, from the evidence of its success in establishing front groups capable of mustering large numbers of peasants or workers for a street rally or a *toma,* and in building up guerrilla bases both in Santiago and the provinces, that the MIR transformed itself from an isolated group of middle-class would-be guerrillas into a serious revolutionary movement between 1970 and 1973. Its relations with the Marxist government might be compared to those between the 'Guevarist' movement of peasants and rural intellectuals that was crushed by Mrs Banadaranaike's government of Communists and Trotskyists after a short-lived insurgency in Ceylon early in 1971.

Towards the end, Allende may have come to regard the MIR and workers' brigades as a force he could use against the regular army if it turned against him. He was only ready to act firmly against left-wing extremists on two occasions during his first two years in office: in June 1971, after the murder of Eduardo Pérez Zújovic, when the VOP was relentlessly tracked down by the police and officially declared to have been 'destroyed'; and a little more than a year later, when the '16th July Commando' plotted to attack the president's own house. In the months before the coup, the army successfully pressed for determined arms searches, which resulted in violent clashes in the southern province of Punta

Areanas and in Santiago itself. But Allende could never agree to military demands to clean up the guerrilla bases, still less to outlaw the MIR.

In the tangled undergrowth of extremist politics in Chile, there are a number of other potential terrorist groups similar to these, with loose connections with both the Socialist Party and the MIR. But the MIR is the one with the training, the popular backing, and the disciplined leadership to function as Chile's *Tupamaros* when times changed and it was forced to operate in clandestinity. Ironically, many of the *mirista* predictions about the course of events under Allende proved to be prophetic. In the end, the middle-class was ready to fight rather than see itself destroyed, and the armed forces were ready to fight rather than see their role usurped by an emerging revolutionary militia. The MIR was itself a major catalyst in the process that brought Allende down, but it is unlikely to profit from it.

Notes to this chapter are on page 212

CHAPTER SIX

The Opposition Mobilises

Towards a United Opposition

The forces within both the government and the opposition were warring among themselves over most of the period up to the March 1973 election. The opposition leaders were slow to draw the obvious conclusion from the election that had brought Allende to power: that, despite the fact that they commanded majority support in the country, they could not block the Marxist programme without forming a united front. But it was a considerable achievement that the opposition parties that made up the Democratic Confederation (CODE) looked much less divided than the Marxists by the time of the March elections. Ironically, Fidel Castro was one of those who helped to consolidate this alliance of opposition parties. During his visit to Chile in November 1971, he had attacked the entire opposition to Allende as 'Fascists'—which stung many Christian Democrats into sinking their differences with the Nationals.

The reasons for the mutual distrust of the Nationals and the Christian Democrats after the 1970 election are not hard to locate. Their leaders were divided both by class and conviction. The Nationalists were widely regarded as the traditional right, the party of the landowners and industrialists represented in the National Society of Agriculture (SNA) and the Chilean Chamber of Commerce, although under the leadership of Sergio Onofre Jarpa they developed both a more ideological bent and a broader popular appeal. The Christian Democrats, in contrast, were much more heterogeneous in

J

their social origins, a party of the lower middle class, of civil servants and (increasingly) of peasants and workers, committed to a 'non-capitalist' model of development. The Nationals blamed the Christian Democrats for opening the way for Allende in 1970, and in return, the Christian Democrat Left quoted Tomic's notorious aphorism: 'If you win with the right, it is the right that wins.'

An additional problem was the temptation for many Christian Democrats to acquiesce in Allende's 'middle strategy'. There was much talk at the end of 1970 that Allende would actually try to draw the party—or Tomic's section of it—into the Popular Unity government. As far as one can tell, no formal offer was actually made, although it proved expedient to encourage the ambitions of individual Christian Democrat leaders.

Nevertheless, the Christian Democrats and the Nationals found themselves increasingly in agreement on three basic issues: the government's disrespect for the country's democratic institutions; its assault on private property (and its lack of regard for the concept of workers' participation promoted by the Christian Democrats); and its unwillingness to control the spread of violence. The catalyst that brought the two parties together was the second major political assassination since the 1970 election—a murder as important in its effects as the Schneider killing and compared at the time, slightly inaccurately, to the murder of Calvo Sotelo before the Spanish Civil War. Edmundo Pérez Zújovic was prominent in the conservative faction of the Christian Democrat Party, and had served as Frei's minister of the interior. On 8 July 1971, he was machine-gunned to death as he drove to his office. His killers were members of the far-left People's Organised Vanguard (VOP) and one of their leaders was among the prisoners who had received an amnesty when Allende took office. Although Allende ordered the police to crack down on the VOP in a spectacular man-hunt, ex-president Frei argued that the murder had demonstrated the failure of the government to restrain the violence of the extreme left.

Partly as a result of the killing, the Christian Democrat candidate in the Valparaiso by-election in July was allowed to accept the support of the local Nationals. The result was an opposition success. Despite the government's efforts to buy electoral support by handing out interest-free loans after an earthquake that rocked Valparaiso a few weeks before polling day, the Christian Democrat pulled in just over half of the votes cast.

Not everyone in Frei's party was happy with this result. The left-wing faction headed by Bosco Parra and supported by the leader of the party's youth movement later tried to persuade the party council to prohibit any kind of understanding, formal or informal, with the National Party. When this proposal was rejected in favour of a resolution attacking the 'totalitarian and exclusive spirit' of the Allende government, Bosco Parra, several youth leaders, and eight deputies left the party to form a new group, the Christian Left (*Izquierda Cristiana*). Chonchol and some of the earlier generation of Christian Democrat rebels who had founded the MAPU left their own party to join the Christian Left.

The split was not serious enough to destroy the position of the Christian Democrats as Chile's biggest single party. On the other hand, by shedding some of the doubters on the left, the pro-Frei faction of the party was able to move further towards a tactical alliance with the Nationals. The worsening economic situation and the continuing diatribes in the pro-government press against Frei prompted the party's secretary-general, Renán Fuentealba, to deliver a stinging attack on the Allende regime in September. He accused the Allende government of violating the Statute of Guarantees, of resorting to illegal methods in order to take over private firms, and of creating a 'climate of hatred' that incited personal defamation and even assassination. He warned that his party was now determined to use 'the legal and constitutional instruments available to us in order to force the government to fulfil the promises that it has freely agreed to'.[1]

It was not an idle threat. The Christian Democrats (who

had earlier refused to support a move by the Nationals to impeach the economics minister) now put forward a constitutional amendment to check the power of the executive to take over private businesses. This amendment, or 'law on the three areas' was introduced by Juan Hamilton and Renán Fuentealba late in October 1971. Its key points were that no further expropriations of private enterprises should take place without specific legislation by Congress; the government would be allowed to intervene in a business (in accordance with Decree-Law 520) only if production had stopped for more than twenty days and it was proved that the management was at fault; and the purchase of shares by the government after 14 October was to be declared null and void. The effect of this amendment, of course, would have been to strip the government of most of the powers it had used to expand its hold over the private sector of the economy.

But Allende applied his presidential veto after Congress adopted the amendment by a simple majority in February 1972. When the opposition leaders protested that a two-thirds majority was not required to secure its passage and that the Constitutional Tribunal (appointed by Allende) was not qualified to rule on the issue,[2] Allende refused to give way. The dispute over this amendment resulted in the most serious clash between the president and parliament during Allende's first two years. Its outcome was also the prime example of the impotence of Congress in its attempts to curb the state takeover of private industry.

The Nationals welcomed the Hamilton–Fuentealba amendment, and backed the Christian Democrats when they moved to impeach the minister of the interior, Jose Tohá, on a variety of charges. In a major speech before a vast audience gathered in the National Stadium on 16 December, Fuentealba attacked the minister for failing to take action against armed extremists, for violating the right of free assembly (by preventing peasant groups from attending a rally) and for discriminating against the independent media. He expressed sympathy with the housewives who had been attacked by young Socialists and *miristas* during their demonstration against food shortages and rising prices. And he made a caustic summary of the general drift of government policy:

> The people of Chile reject the attempt of the minority in power ... to build against their will a new order that bears no resemblance to the Chilean style of socialism ... which is free, pluralistic and democratic ... since each day warns us more and more clearly that these very unoriginal rulers of ours want to copy the socialist systems that have been imposed on other countries ... What are we witnessing? It is a dark process, often taking place at the margin of the law, that is creating the bases for a treacherous kind of socialism that is incompatible with the democratic system.[3]

The language of the Christian Democrats was now much closer to that of the Nationals, who had warned from the beginning of the threat to Chile's democratic institutions implicit in the Marxist programme. Tohá was duly impeached by Congress in January, but Allende avoided dropping him from the cabinet by switching him to the ministry of defence —a game of musical chairs that was played out again in July, when the opposition parties brought another censure motion against Tohá's successor, Hernán del Canto. It was not until April 1973, that the opposition parties gave thought to the possibility of impeaching the entire cabinet, which could have made it impossible for Allende to save individual ministers by switching their portfolios.

The greater unity of the parliamentary opposition did not enable Congress to take effective measures to control the executive. By the end of 1971, in fact, it had become clear that the system of checks and balances (between executive, legislature and judiciary) had broken down. On the first day of 1972, for example, the opposition voted to cut the government's proposed budget by some $306 million—a measure designed to cut off the funds used by CORFO to buy up shares as well as to bring the current account deficit within reasonable bounds. Allende vetoed the bill and then passed it on to the Constitutional Tribunal (in which the three government appointees outnumbered the two Supreme Court judges). On 19 January, predictably, this court ruled that the budget cuts were unconstitutional. Congress was a little more successful later in the year in forcing the government to take action against the armed groups on the left. A bill sponsored by the Christian Democrat senator, Juan de Dios Carmona, was designed to make the army responsible for controlling the possession of arms in the country. Private citizens were to apply to local garrison commanders for the licence to hold guns, and the army was to police the new regulations. Allende moved to veto the bill, but it was subsequently established that his veto had been 'improperly put'; on these technical grounds, the Dios Carmona bill became law in October.

But in general, it would be accurate to say that the role of the parliamentary opposition was at best a negative one. Except in the special case of the copper nationalisation bill, Allende was forced to justify his executive actions on the basis of existing legislation, since it was impossible to have new enabling laws passed. But Congress was then shown to be almost entirely ineffective as a filter for executive action—despite government complaints of 'reactionary obstructionism'.

The most dramatic rewards of the new entente between the Nationals and the Christian Democrats came in the by-elections held in January 1972 for the senate seat of O'Higgins and Colchagua and the seat of Linares. The parties agreed to support Rafael Moreno (a young and highly energetic Christian Democrat who had once earned the National's dislike as head of CORA under Frei but was now moving towards the conservative wing of the party) for the senate seat and Sergio Diez (a popular and media-conscious National who later became an effective champion of small farmers threatened by *tomas* and official expropriation) in

Linares. The government mounted a major propaganda offen-
sive in both areas. Moreno's liberal past made a nonsense of
official attempts to represent the Christian Democrats as a
'party of reaction' but he had to do battle in a mining and
farming region where the left had polled strongly in the
1971 municipal elections. As it turned out, however, both
Moreno and Diez won comfortably; Moreno got 52.7 per
cent of the vote and Diez got 58 per cent.

These results were a tremendous blow to the government's
morale and resulted in the soul-searching that produced the
Arrayán statement and a partial change of strategy intended
to win back the support of the 'middle sectors'. The moderates who had broken away from the Radical Party in protest
at its Marxist leanings and founded the PIR were now
induced to return to the cabinet. Even more important, in
the months that followed, Allende attempted to hold out an
olive branch to the Christian Democrats. He involved them
in two rounds of negotiations on the Hamilton–Fuentealba
amendment. In March, the minister of justice, Dr Manuel
Sanhueza (PIR) was instructed to seek a compromise formula.
He seemed to be on the brink of an agreement with the
Christian Democrats when other members of the government
(notably the Socialists) objected violently to the idea of
restricting the powers of the executive to take over private
firms, and the PIR withdrew from the cabinet.

Allende then made a violent speech in which he threatened
to dissolve Congress if it persisted in its 'obstructionist attitudes towards the executive'. Although he dropped hints to
foreign correspondents about his willingness to hold a plebiscite on a new constitution, it was perfectly clear that—on
the basis of recent election results—he could have no confidence in his chances of winning. Instead, as it transpired,
Allende made new advances to the Christian Democrats.
Fuentealba authorised a team of Christian Democrats including Tomás Pablo and Felipe Amunategui to enter into negotiations with government representatives on the night of 12
June—other party leaders privately claimed that he had done

so without consulting the party council. These talks finally broke down on 29 June, when it became clear that Allende was not prepared to give guarantees for the survival of the *Papelera* or of four private banks, which the Christian Democrats had originally wished to see preserved in the form of workers' co-operatives.

That marked the definitive parting of the ways between the Popular Unity government and the Christian Democratic Party. The voices of those in Frei's party who had been ready to underwrite at least part of the Marxist experiment were now barely audible. The Nationals and the Christian Democrats again joined forces to contest the Coquimbo by-election in July. This time, the Communist candidate, 'Amandita' Altamirano, was victorious, in an area that had always been a stronghold of the Marxist parties. But it did not go unnoticed that the Popular Unity's share of the total vote dropped by some 8 per cent. The government continued to lose ground in the university and union elections as well.

The four main opposition groups were able, later that year, to set up the *Confederación Democratica* (CODE) to contest the March 1973 elections. This grouped together the Christian Democrats, the Nationals, the Radical Democrats, and the PIR. But the opposition leaders remained divided over the purpose of the CODE; while conservatives and *freistas* hoped that it would provide a fairly permanent basis for joint action, left-wing Christian Democrats preferred to see it as a temporary, tactical arrangement that would come to an end after the elections.

The Role of the Media

Throughout this confused period of political realignment, the press played a critical role. After more than two years of the Allende government, visitors to Santiago were still surprised by the variety and combative nature of the Chilean press. Chile is one of the few countries in Latin America where the free press has functioned as an effective watchdog for democratic liberties. Early in 1973, it was still possible to choose at the news-stands between half a dozen morning papers, ranging from the government mouthpiece *La Nación* and the Communist organ *El Siglo* to the Christian Democrat *La Prensa* (founded in 1970) the independent conservative *El Mercurio* and the National Party's *La Tribuna*. There were still four or five afternoon papers, and more than a dozen major weeklies ranging from serious news magazines like *Que Pasa* or *Ercilla* to the polemical literature of the far left and the far right and the government's *conzientizado* publications—an almost untranslatable word that applies to its instruments in the campaign of political 'conscientisation'.

The inquisitiveness and fierce independence of Chilean journalists, both in the press and in broadcasting, was a thorn in the side of the Allende government and one of the guarantees of the survival of democratic institutions. The importance of a journal like *El Mercurio* in tackling the government on every controversial issue and in sustaining the morale of the opposition can hardly be exaggerated. There is no doubt that the Marxist parties would have moved further and faster towards their ultimate goals but for the many spotlights that were trained on them. The independence of the press, unfortunately, is not a principle that figures prominently in the statutes of any existing Communist society, and the Chilean Marxists gave an inkling of what it meant to them in the course of the 'Assembly of Journalists of the Left' that was held in Santiago in April 1971. At this meeting, the president of the organising committee, Manuel Cabieses (the extremist director of *Punto Final*) declared that 'the basic duty of the journalist is to subject himself to the class struggle'. Felidor Contreras, the Communist secretary of the same committee, added the reflection that the duty of all journalists of the left was to give total support to the government of Popular Unity.[4] The delegates reached consensus in their final resolutions, which declared that objectivity in journalism does not exist; 'the only truly objective journalist is the one who identifies himself with the great historical revolutionary process that at this time is shaking the whole

world and has raised its victorious banner in our country'.[5]

How did the government interpret these principles in
practice? There had been threats of direct interference with
the opposition press during the election campaign, when
Allende talked of expropriating *El Mercurio* (which supported Alessandri in the 1970 election). But the suppression
of the country's oldest and most powerful newspaper—or
formal censorship of the press in general—was not an immediate possibility for the new government. Moves of this nature
would have aroused bitter opposition and would have suggested that the government was moving in an anti-democratic
direction. Apart from those general considerations, Allende's
coalition had promised to respect the Statute of Guarantees
that had been passed by Congress on 22 October 1970. The
Christian Democrats who drew up these constitutional guarantees had taken care to provide in detail for safeguards for
the freedom of the press. At the time that they were passed
into law, Allende had declared that he would respect them
as 'a moral law before our conscience and before history'.
But fine phrases are quickly forgotten in politics. A few
months later, he was shrugging off the Statute of Guarantees
in his dialogue with Régis Debray as merely 'a tactical necessity'.

How were these pledges for the freedom of the means of
communication actually observed? It is worth running briefly
through the list. One of the key clauses in the Statute provided that all political parties would enjoy 'free access' to the
government-controlled media. (Article 9.4). In fact, the state
television network (Channel 7) was rapidly turned into a
channel for Marxist propaganda, and the one current-affairs
programme on national television that gave opposition politicians a chance to put their case ('A Tres Bandas') was sup-
pressed in August, 1971. The government newspaper, *La
Nación*, became simply a mouthpiece for the regime, while
some of its employees were later found to be turning out
'parallel publications' like *Tarea Urgente*, a broadsheet for

the ultras of the industrial *cordones*. The new government-controlled publishing house, Editorial Quimantú, confined itself to printing Marxist literature.

The Statute also upheld the freedom to publish or broadcast without prior censorship. (Article 10.3). Yet, during the wave of strikes in October 1972—a period of tremendous confusion and grave social crisis—the voice of the non-governmental radio stations was silenced, and all radio stations were ordered to broadcast only the transmissions of the official agency OIR (Oficina de Radiodifusíón de la Presidencia de la República). The Statute upheld the right of reply for those who were 'offended by any information' put out in the press, on radio or on television. (Article 10.3). Yet both ex-president Frei and Eduardo Boeninger, the rector of the University of Chile, were denied the right of reply to serious allegations made about them on government television. The Statute contained another key clause defending the 'free import and sale' of paper, machinery, spare parts and other necessary equipment for the maintenance of the means of communication. (Article 10.3). This was not respected either. The state development corporation, CORFO, proceeded to set up a monopoly of the import and distribution of equipment and replacements for radio transmitters, while the Central Bank denied Channel 13 (which belongs to the Catholic University) the foreign exchange to buy a new transmitter from abroad.[6] As far as the press was concerned, the Statute was a dead letter.

These were some of the lesser pressures that the independent media were subjected to. The government in fact had some more powerful weapons at its disposal for bringing the press to heel. These included: orchestrating labour unrest or the seizure of plant by left-wing ultras; discrimination against individual papers or the non-government television station (by denying press conferences or the right to broadcast to the whole country); juggling with prices and wages so as to drive a target-enterprise into financial difficulties. The most effective measure of all was financial asphyxiation. It became in-

creasingly doubtful whether the finance would continue to
be available to support opposition papers and radio stations
as the revenue from commercial advertising fell away with the
extension of state control over private industries.

Little could be hoped for from the new government adver-
tisers. Allende refused to accept a bill tabled by the Christian
Democrats in 1971 that would have required official adver-
tisers to share out their commissions among the press on an
equitable basis. It was later established that the bulk of
government advertising was channelled through four separate agencies, each of which was controlled by a party in the
Popular Unity coalition: Agencia Territorio was run by the
Communists, and distributed advertising for COHABIT
and Sumar, among many other companies; Agencia Vanguardia was run by the Socialists and represented, *inter alia*,
CODELCO and the Banco del Estado; Agencia Latina fell
to the Radicals; and Agencia Stentor to API, which also
somehow managed to get a slice of the cake.[7] The obvious
effect of this political re-structuring of the advertising business in Chile was that left-wing papers that had previously
been almost empty of advertisements became fatter overnight, while the advertising revenues of the local equiva-
lents of the *New York Times* or the *Daily Telegraph*
dwindled to a fraction of their former level. To an orthodox
Marxist, this must have appeared a text-book example of
the relationship between 'infrastructure' and 'superstructure'; change the economic 'infrastructure', and it is only a
matter of time before the 'superstructure' of ideas and
opinions will also change.

Pro-government publications could count on money transferred from expropriated firms as well as official advertising
to keep them afloat. It was established, late in 1972, that
money from the El Teniente mine had been used to help
finance a number of new periodicals as well as the new state
publishing firm, Quimantú.[8]

Two special targets were *El Mercurio* and the *Papelera*
(or *Campania Manufacturera de Papeles y Cartones*) the only

private source of newsprint in Chile. Both *El Mercurio* and *Papelera* managed to survive during the whole span of the Allende government; but the tactics used against them are a fair sample of the methods used by the Marxist parties in their efforts to curb their critics. *El Mercurio,* the independent newspaper founded by the Edwards family in Valparaiso early in the last century, enjoys a special place in Latin-American journalism: it has been a continuous publication for longer than any other paper in the Spanish-speaking world. It was always one of Allende's *bêtes noires,* and after his election, he pursued a running debate with the paper, writing long letters to the editor and making frequent accusations that the paper had distorted the facts. The paper was frequently singled out as a 'class enemy' in the Communist Party press, and on his return from his Latin-American tour in September 1971, Allende claimed that its publisher, Agustín Edwards (then living in exile in the United States) deserved to be jailed for embezzlement.

The government initially set out to discredit *El Mercurio* by claiming that it had wrongfully accepted a $1 million loan from the First National Bank of Wisconsin; it was subsequently established that this loan had, in accordance with standard practice, been registered with the Central Bank. It also tried to prove that the paper was linked with other companies in the Edwards group (and in particular, with the Banco Edwards) on a financial basis, which is illegal under Chilean law. This was never formally proved, although a special team of investigators was set up to look for evidence of financial transfers. In January 1971, the government took direct action against the paper, to explore alleged tax irregularities. Government inspectors moved into the offices of *El Mercurio* to examine the books and remove files and many other documents essential to the day-to-day running of the paper. They failed in their basic mission, since they were unable to find any pretext to close the paper down, but they presented a bill for 21 million escudos that were said to be owing to the internal revenue service. Although the management immediately filed an appeal, Allende made great play of the alleged delay in paying taxes in a new attack on the paper at the end of that month.

The Marxists now tried a new tactic. They set out to foment labour unrest among the paper's 1,400 employees. A committee supporting the Popular Unity government (CUP) had been set up soon after the 1970 election, with the backing of Sonia Edwards, the sister of the paper's biggest shareholder and a close friend of Carlos Altamirano, the Socialist leader. At the beginning of March 1971, the leader of the CUP, Sergio Gutierrez, demanded equal rights with management for workers in the administration of the paper, its editorial policy and its finances. Nothing came of this, but Gutierrez and his committee joined in a savage campaign against *El Mercurio* in the government-oriented press.

In a message to *La Nación* the following September, for example, the CUP leaders accused the paper's managers and senior editors of 'financial delinquency' and quoted figures for their salaries.[9] This was the last straw for the management. On 10 September, a mass meeting of the paper's employees gave their support for the expulsion of five leaders of the CUP. By this time, the CUP had failed to recruit more than 23 of the paper's 470 employees in Santiago. All the same, the nation-wide 'Assembly of Journalists of the Left' —a Popular Unity front—organised protests and demonstrations in which journalists from other papers took part. And the sacking of the CUP leaders led to fresh attacks on *El Mercurio* from the Communist-led trade union federation. Allende spoke to the union leaders on 15 September and publicly declared himself to be on the side of the men who had been fired and claimed (without any basis whatsoever) that 'the greatest fraud that had taken place in Chile in recent years' had been committed by *El Mercurio*. Hostile crowds gathered outside the paper's grey-stone offices, just behind the supreme court, but a majority of the staff remained loyal, and *El Mercurio* rode out the storm.

But, like the remainder of the free press, *El Mercurio* was subject to steadily mounting economic pressures. Its advertising revenue dropped by 40 per cent in the first three months after the Allende administration took office. The vast amount of campaign advertising carried by the paper during the run-up to the March 1973 elections did not help to recoup its earlier losses, since *El Mercurio* was the victim of an old law retained by the Allende government that fixed the rates for political advertising at an artificially low level which meant, in a period of high inflation, that the prices charged did not even cover the printing costs. Nor could the paper's management count on bank lending to help balance the books after the government nationalised the credit system. In a country with a history of high inflation like Chile, short-term bank lending has provided most of the essential working capital for private companies, including newspapers. From the middle of 1971, the paper could no longer count on private loans.

In addition to these economic strains—only partially countered by the private sacrifices of those employees who contributed 20 per cent of their salaries to keep *El Mercurio* running—the paper had to contend with the constant harassment of individual members of its staff. This ranged from threatening letters and telephone calls to attacks on personal property (like the burning of journalists' cars) to arrest and trial of executives on trumped-up charges of tax evasion. Perhaps because of its continuing prestige and influence, *El Mercurio* did not suffer the occupation of its premises by left-wing extremists or the arbitrary detention of key editorial staff—but those things happened to some less prominent opposition papers.

From one point of view, the *Papelera* was an even more crucial target than *El Mercurio* for those who wished to silence the government's critics in the press. If it passed into the hands of the state, the independent press would have to turn to the government for their supply of newsprint; even the possibility of getting alternative supplies from abroad was dubious, because of official import restrictions and the highly selective way in which the Central Bank, under Communist direction, exercised its powers to control the availability of foreign exchange. Furthermore, since the president of the *Papelera* was Jorge Alessandri, Allende's conservative opponent in the 1970 election, it was difficult for the left-wing press to single out the company as a 'class enemy'.

Rumours that the government was planning to expropriate the *Papelera* began to circulate soon after Allende took office. They were confirmed when the deputy minister of economy, Oscar Garretón, announced in June 1971 that the company would be nationalised within one year. The government tried initially to buy control of the company in the way that it had bought control of many of the banks, by offering to buy the shares of the *Papelera*'s 16,500 shareholders at several times the current market price. CORFO, the state development corporation, was granted the finance to buy stock in the *Papelera* and other private companies on 12 October. The money made available totalled more than 871 million escudos—a curious deployment of 'development funds'. Simultaneously, CORFO launched a propaganda campaign designed to blacken the image of the *Papelera* by representing it as a sinister 'monopoly' that had mistreated its workers and had failed to increase production or manage its resources efficiently. The management of the *Papelera* countered these charges effectively by proving that, over the period between 1956 and 1970, it had invested some $130 million in Chile, boosted its exports by almost 100 per cent per annum (on average) and lifted production by a total of 715 per cent. The management's astute publicity campaign helped to dissuade shareholders from selling out to CORFO.

In mid-November, the so-called 'Fund for Liberty' was also launched to compete with the government in purchasing shares from those determined to sell.[10] By 26 November, it was established that while CORFO had been able to purchase some 3 million shares (out of a total of 145 million), the 'Fund for Liberty' had done rather better: it had bought up 3·2 million. Six months after CORFO was authorised to buy shares in the *Papelera,* the government had still managed to acquire only 7·7 per cent of the stock. This time, private shareholders had apparently put the freedom of the press above their immediate personal interests. It was an important example that was to influence many of the shareholders in private companies that were scheduled for expropriation in 1972.

When its first tactic failed, the government tried a different method. Marxist cells in the *Papelera* tried to stir up labour unrest. But the company was also able to counter this effectively by organising a free ballot in 11 of the 17 syndicates within the enterprise, in which nearly 82 per cent of its employees voted against state takeover and only 12 per cent voted in favour of nationalisation. Many of the *Papelera*'s employees became members of the *gremialista* movement, an independent union movement that grew out of a student organisation at the Catholic University and rapidly gained importance in 1972. The *gremialistas* later staged other demonstrations of workers' opposition to state control. The wives of the men employed in the *Papelera* also played an important part in helping to set up a self-defence group to guard against the possibility that the company premises would be seized by left-wing extremists, as had happened to newspapers and radio stations in the south.

In the face of this impressive display of worker–shareholder solidarity, the government switched to yet another tack. It tried to bankrupt the *Papelera* by refusing to allow the company to raise its prices while costs soared because of statutory wage increases and the higher tariffs charged by public sector service industries. By June 1972, the real price of the company's products had dropped to only half of their 1958 price, and the business was losing about 3 million escudos *a day*. Persistent appeals for an increase in prices were ignored by DIRINCO, the government's price-fixing agency, although it was written in the agency's own statutes that it was required to take account of the 'legitimate profit margin' of the producer. In October 1972, the *Papelera* an-

K

nounced that its losses during the previous financial year had amounted to 228 million escudos and that its 1972 losses would probably total 400 million escudos.[11] It was forced to default on a loan from the World Bank. It was only the resoluteness of its shareholders and employees, and the tremendous campaign on its behalf in the free press, that had enabled it to survive that long. After the military joined the cabinet in November, the company gained a temporary reprieve—an authorised price rise of 45 per cent. But the battle was not over, and it was clear that its final outcome would determine whether or not the government would be able to exercise a stranglehold over the free press.

Many other examples might be taken of the pressures brought to bear on the press: the arbitrary detention of opposition editors (like Mario Carneyro, of *La Segunda,* or Maximiniano Errazuriz, of *El Condor,* a Santa Cruz paper); the unjustified closure of local radio stations; the attempts to prevent the only genuinely independent television station, Channel 13, from extending its network across the country—which went as far as deliberate interference with its broadcasting equipment. Some readers may be surprised, not that these attempts were made, but that they fell so far short of their goal. The point is that the Allende government was fighting a war of attrition, confident that—over a period of several years—the economic resources needed to sustain the independent press would be exhausted.

Class War and 'Class Law'

Just as Chile's Marxists knew nothing and cared less about objectivity in journalism (or scholarship) so they totally rejected the concept of 'even-handed justice.' The government was committed to substituting 'socialist legality' for 'bourgeois legality.' This meant that the existing judiciary would be swept away when conditions made that possible and would be replaced by a system of tribunals responsible to a new 'people's assembly' and (at a local level) to neighbourhood committees. This new form of 'class justice' would differ from Chile's traditional legal system in three significant ways. First, the classical distinction between the judiciary, the legislature and the executive would be swept away. Second, the concept of defence of the individual and his private property would be replaced by a collectivist concept; good or bad would finally become identifiable with what served the interests of the socialist state and what undermined it. Finally, the administration of the law would no longer be carried out according to objective norms, but according to ideology. The basic safeguards for individual rights would disappear.

A foretaste of what form this 'socialist legality' might take was provided by the government's proposals for a bill to establish a system of neighbourhood tribunals in January 1971. These new courts were to be elected at a local level; the judges could only be removed by the will of two-thirds of the residents. The vague definitions of the crimes they were supposed to punish left enormous scope for arbitrary action or political persecution; for example, they were to deal with 'attempts against wholesome co-existence in family and community'—a mandate that was compared to an article in the Nazi penal code which made it possible to punish any act 'against wholesome public sentiment'. Vague charges of this kind, that failed to fix specific penalties for specific crimes, contravened the accepted legal norms in all open societies by leaving so much scope for arbitrary rulings on non-existent crimes. The Allende government's draft bill also contained some other unsettling elements: those summoned before neighbourhood courts would not be allowed defence attorneys, and, if found guilty, they might be subjected to a range of humiliating petty punishments more appropriate to a society where public self-criticism sessions are routine than to a democratic country—such as forced labour on holidays, public apologies that might be broadcast on radio and television, and so on. The bill was never actually brought before Congress, since it became clear that all opposition parties would vote solidly against it. But it provided a few clues to the Marxist conception of law in Chile.

The preceding chapters have shown how Allende was forced to work within the existing legal framework, since he lacked the strength in Congress to pass new laws on divisive issues and lacked the majority strength in the country that might have enabled him to change the constitution by plebiscite. Because of the wide-ranging powers that he enjoyed as president under the 1925 constitution, and because of the skill of his main legal advisers—notably Eduardo Novoa and José Antonio Viera Gallo, the *mapucista* under-secretary for justice who was the real force at the ministry of justice under a series of ministers—Allende was able to put Congress and the courts on the defensive from quite early on. The legal institution that perhaps gave him the greatest trouble was the Contraloría (a word that might be clumsily translated as the Office of the Auditor-General). Originally set up in 1927[12] to keep a check on the government's financial transactions, the Contraloría had wide-ranging powers to pass judgment on the legality of government decrees and to supervise the conduct of the administration.

The man who remained auditor-general throughout Allende's time in power was Hector Humeres—austere, respected and not easily intimidated. He maintained the independence of his office, blocked—at least temporarily—the unjustified takeover of a number of private firms, and insisted on the principle that government intervention under the terms of the decree-law of 1932 was a purely temporary measure and that the companies affected must be returned to their owners in due course. But his rulings were not final. As has been seen, the Contraloría was overruled twenty-eight times by a 'decree of insistence' signed by all members of the cabinet before the military entered the government in November.

In July 1972, a mob gathered in the Plaza Montt-Varas in Santiago, threatening three neighbouring buildings: Con-

gress, the Supreme Court, and the offices of *El Mercurio*.
Among the street-orators who stood up to attack all three
institutions as 'centres of counter-revolution' (and, in the
case of the newspaper, as 'the central committee of the
bourgeoisie') were the intendant of Santiago, Alfredo Joignant, the Socialist leader Hernán del Canto, who had been
minister of the interior until the previous day, when he
was impeached by Congress, and a rising young Socialist
extremist called Rolandó Calderón.[13] Their fiery words, and
the strongly-worded letters exchanged between the Supreme
Court and the minister of justice afterwards,[14] might have
suggested that the Chilean left had been deeply frustrated
by the obstacles to the revolutionary process that parliament
and the courts had presented. Certainly, things would have
moved much faster if Allende had enjoyed a majority in
Congress and been able to name his Supreme Court.

But the main lesson of Allende's first two years for the
Chilean opposition was the impotence of Congress and the
courts in the face of executive action. This encouraged the
growth of extra-parliamentary resistance movements, ranging from spontaneous housewives' demonstration to organised strike action and the occupation of school buildings
or university faculties by militant opposition students'
groups. It contributed to the rapid growth of the *gremialista*
movement, an independent union movement that attempted
to group together private business, professional groups, and
ordinary workers on the basis of a philosophy of 'co-participation' in industry. Perhaps the *gremialista* movement is
best compared with the phenomenon of Poujadism in France
in the 1950s. Like the Poujadists, the *gremialistas* were
essentially a movement of little people—of shopkeepers,
truckdrivers, small and middling farmers and professional
groups of doctors, lawyers and engineers—a movement of
those whose lives and livelihoods were invested in Chile and
who had suffered most from the deepening economic crisis
and the steady expansion of state control.

Its beginnings were in the Catholic University, among the

students who eventually won control of the local student federation under the leadership of a brilliant young theologian and political commentator called Jaime Guzmán. Jaime Guzmán also contributed a great deal in the early stages to the development of an ideology and a political programme. But when it came to broadening the bases of the movement, knitting the different groups together and gearing it for action in the wave of strikes that erupted in October, it was a group of highly shrewd organisers from the private sector who counted: Jorge Fontaine, Benjamin Matte of the National Society of Agriculture, and, on a slightly different tack, Orlando Saenz, the combative young president of the industrialists' association (SOFOFA).

At a different level, rising street violence, the new climate of class hatred, and the government's failure to provide police protection against attacks on property by left-wing extremists led to the creation of local vigilante groups. In the south (especially in Cautín) a farmers' self-defence group nicknamed the *Guardia Blanca* (a name that it finally adopted as its own) organised the re-occupation of farms that had been seized illegally. The first of these *retomas* took place at the 'Santa Ana' farm near Lautaro in Cautín in February 1972. (There had, of course, been a number of private enterprise operations earlier on.) I was shown the battle-flags of the MIR captured on that occasion on a visit to Lautaro shortly afterwards. At least temporarily, the emergence of vigilante groups of this kind froze *mirista* operations in the far south, and set a precedent for similar groups in Santiago. Early in 1972, the *Guardia Blanca* in Cautín claimed to remove sixty cars and had little trouble in smuggling guns in across the Argentine border. They also had a discipline that, at that stage, the *miristas* of the area possibly still lacked—partly the contribution of the German–Chilean settlers of the region.[15]

These self-defence groups were not limited to the provinces. A movement called PROTECO was formed in Santiago and probably included some 1,500 reasonably active members by the beginning of 1973; this was basically an organisation of concerned householders who feared attacks on their property and got together to train themselves in self-defence and set up voluntary night patrols to prevent any sudden invasion of their residential areas. On the far right, parliamentary or corporatist organisations like the *Frente Nacionalista Patria y Libertad* and SOL (for *Soberanía, Orden y Libertad*) also won more recruits as the battle-lines hardened. They were certainly no equivalent for the MIR and the Socialist ultras, though *Patria y Libertad* later embarked on a campaign of 'direct action' against the government instigated by its deputy chief, Roberto Thieme. Though the name of Pablo Rodriguez (the movement's leader) appeared constantly in the pro-government press as the harbinger of 'Fascism' in Chile, his concept of the 'corporate state' was pretty confused.

The October Strikes

The full extent of the opposition to the Allende government was revealed in October 1972, when a wave of strikes shook the country. The government's apologists made out that this protest movement was a 'bosses' strike', part of a sinister conspiracy to disrupt the economy and trigger off a miliary coup. But the course of events showed that in fact nothing was carefully planned, and that what began as the spontaneous reaction of southern truck-drivers to a new nationalisation scheme that threatened their livelihoods ended by involving a broad cross-section of Chilean society. The established opposition parties, far from helping to organise the strike action, were caught by surprise and lent their support to it only when it was well under way. As the strike movement gathered force, it involved a startling variety of occupational groups, including high school and university students, shopkeepers and bank clerks, peasants from some 5,000 *asentamientos,* pilots and bus-drivers, merchant seamen and stevedores, and professional groups such as lawyers, doctors and engineers.

It began in the remote southern province of Aysén, with the determined resistance of members of the truck-drivers' federation (*Confederación de Dueños Camioneros*) to attempts to set up a new state-run trucking company. Chile's lorry-drivers are not exactly model *momios*. Like long-distance lorry-drivers in most parts of the world, they are a breed of tough, resourceful and independent men, plying the long Pacific Highway running straight as a plumb-line from north to south. Most of them own their own trucks, which are mostly broken-down Fords or Chevrolets that a hired chauffeur (or so they boast to foreign reporters) wouldn't know how to keep on the road. Their federation, run by an ex-Socialist called León Vilarín, is a grouping of 165 local syndicates with a total of about 40,000 members. Between them, they own 56,000 vehicles—a figure that hardly suggests that this is a 'conspiracy of bosses'.

Trouble between the truck-drivers and the government had been brewing up for some time and threatened to explode in September, when there were threats of a joint strike by three transport federations—the lorry-drivers, taxi-drivers, and bus-drivers. That was averted by a compromise agreement patched together on 12 September. One of the concessions that the government made was to allow the lorry-drivers to raise their tariffs by 120 per cent to keep abreast of inflation. But a few weeks later, they were complaining that the government had failed to keep some of its other promises. In particular, they complained that they could not obtain tyres or spare parts (partly as a result of official import restrictions); that they could not buy new trucks from abroad, although the state corporations were receiving Fiat lorries partly assembled in Casablanca; and that the government was still pressing ahead with its plans to increase state control over the transport sector.

They were not exactly comforted when the minister of economy, Carlos Matus, saw fit to declare that 'the business of transport is too important to be left in the hands of the private sector' and that (in Lenin's words) the nationalisation of transport was essential to 'the construction of socialism'.[16] Matus showed he was serious when plans were announced for the formation of several mixed-ownership trucking companies (with major CORFO participation), while the state copper corporation, CODELCO, was authorised to buy a majority shareholding in the private firm that provided transport for copper shipments from the Chuquicamata mine.[17]

But it was the attempt of the left-wing governor of the far-off southern state of Aysén to set up a trucking company controlled by CORFO that finally goaded the drivers' unions into action. On 9 October, they presented a seven-point petition to Admiral Huerta, who had been made president of the newly-formed National Confederation of Transport. Their major demand was for a halt to the process of state takeover. But the fact that the petition also called for the return of Radio Agricultura de los Angeles to its owners (it had been closed down by the government) and for fair prices for the *Papelera* newsprint corporation was used by the government as a pretext to declare that the union leaders' motives were 'political and anti-professional'. Two days later, the truck-drivers' federation announced a strike.

Carlos Altamirano promptly denounced Leon Vilarín, the 57 year old former Socialist militant who had emerged as the truck-drivers' leader, as a 'traitor'. To which Vilarín replied tartly: 'I was already a Socialist, when Sr Altamirano was a lawyer employed by a North-American company to defend its interests against those of Chile.' The government responded by declaring the strike illegal and clapping Vilarín and some of his fellow-unionists into jail. Vilarín later declared that an attempt had even been made to dupe him and his colleagues into leaving the jail without the proper release documents so that they could be accused of attempted escape.

It soon became clear that the truck-drivers were not without friends. On 13 October, the shopkeepers' federation, led by Rafael Cumsille, also joined the strike. The shopkeepers (who had staged a work stoppage earlier in the year) had plenty of complaints of their own: the strong-arm tactics of the JAPs and the left-wing organisers of the neighbourhood 'people's stores' (*almacenes populares*); favouritism and petty racketeering by officials in the state distribution agencies; illegal seizures of property; the general shortage of food and consumer goods; and a diffuse—but by no means unwarranted —fear of a formal system of rationing. In the days that followed, professional men, students, peasants, harbour employees, pilots and cafe proprietors also lent their weight to the strike, which revealed the increasing polarisation of Chilean society. In contrast, most factory and mine workers stayed at work, as did state employees in the railways.

In a sense, the battle-lines were drawn in Chile in October. But the confrontation could not be viewed in the crude class-oriented terms used by the Marxists. It was not so much a clash between the bourgeoisie and the proletariat (if those terms have any meaning in a country where 80 per cent of the population, if one trusts the public opinion polls, consider themselves to be 'middle class') as between those who felt they had some stake in the new order and those whose interests had suffered. On the side of the strikers, the traditional political parties became deeply involved—the Nationals and the Radical Democrats almost immediately, the Christian Democrats a little later and at first more hesitantly.

It was Frei's personal influence, more than any other factor, that drove the Christian Democrat leaders to declare the 'mobilisation of the bases' in support of the strike. On 15 October, the party's secretary-general Renán Fuentealba, declared:

The fact that this government is acting openly in defiance of the constitution and the laws, as well as of fundamental human rights, is dangerous for all our citizens. The case of the truck-drivers is a striking example. This is a union of working men, and because of the mere fact that [its leaders] protested against what they considered to be an attack on their source of employment, the government accused them of playing politics and flung them into jail. Is it playing politics to oppose this government when it tries to destroy a union in order to make way for a state enterprise?[18]

The leaders of the National Party saw the strike as one of the few remaining means of resisting the drift towards the total concentration of power in the hands of the Marxist parties. 'Organised civil resistance,' the Party's original statement declared, 'maintained on all fronts, is the only effective way of preventing the transformation of Chile into a dependency of the communist world.'

The opposition parties maintained a united front throughout the strikes. But the strike movement itself was not created in the committee rooms. It began at the grassroots, and the impromptu co-ordinating committee that took form as the *comando gremial* was not an assembly of old-style politicians, but of union leaders, industrialists, professional men and student organisers, often meeting in the offices of Radio Agricultura, which played a key part throughout the strike, and later came to describe itself as the 'voice of the *gremios*'. The government took this coalition of forces seriously enough to resort to extraordinary measures, starting with the declaration of a partial state of emergency on 13 October that was soon extended to 21 of Chile's 25 provinces. General Hector Bravo, responsible for the Santiago area as the local garrison commander, issued a decree providing for the seizure of the trucks and shops belonging to those who joined the strike. Five union leaders were imprisoned.

The armed forces were also made responsible for imposing a rigid system of censorship over the country's 125 radio stations. A new decree requiring all radio stations to transmit the propaganda put out by the official broadcasting network, OIR, was bitterly contested both by the opposition parties and by the broadcasters' association, ARCHI. In fact, there is reason for thinking that this decree was highly controversial within the armed forces themselves, and was executed only after a heated internal debate in which General Prats took the government's side. Several Santiago radio stations (including Agricultura, Balmaceda and Yungay—associated with the *gremios*, the Christian Democrats and the Radical Left Party) suffered temporary closure for failure to obey the censorship decree. They continued to broadcast the sounds of OIR officials as they entered the studios—significantly, the army left it to the officials to do the dirty work.

Although an estimated 250,000 people joined in the 'day of silence' in sympathy with the strikers on 24 October, the 'national strike' failed to bring the country to a halt, and Allende very cleverly engineered a situation in which those who had stopped work appeared to be lined up against the men in uniform instead of their real target—the government. The strike leaders issued their terms on 21 October. The self-styled *comando gremial* confronted the government with a list of far-reaching demands that challenged its entire programme. These included: the restitution of businesses expropriated since 21 August; the promulgation of the Hamilton–Fuentealba bill; the suppression of the JAPs; the expulsion of foreign extremists from the country; just prices for the *Papelera*; an end to radio censorship; and the promise of no reprisals against those who had participated in the strike. This manifesto amounted to rather more than a *cahier des doléances*. It was a call to the government, in effect, to apply the brakes to the whole process that the Marxist strategy of building up political power through the assault on the private sector had set in motion. Allende refused to negotiate on this basis.

He managed, instead, to find a rather unusual way out. The situation by the end of October presented him with a number of options. While it was clear that the strike movement had seriously damaged the economy (the government later claimed that the cost amounted to some $270 million) it had not brought the country to a halt. The strike leaders had noticeably failed to enlist the support of the industrial workers, some of whom were organised by Socialist left-wingers and *miristas* to carry out illegal seizures of shops and businesses that had closed down. By the end of the strike, some 150 businesses had been seized (legally or illegally) and a third of these were later formally expropriated. The appearance of disciplined assault-parties from the industrial *cordones* encouraged some of the ultras within Popular Unity to argue that the time had come to 'finish the revolution'. Allende himself was ready to boast to a group of foreign correspondents on 21 October (ten days after the truck-drivers came out on strike) that:

It would only take one word from me to bring 15,000 or 20,000 workers from the industrial fringes of Santiago to come and reopen the shops that have closed down. We told them no. The strength of this government is in its respect for the constitution and the law.

By this stage, Allende and his ministers had been able to measure the challenge posed by the strikers and had partially overcome their initial fears. A few days earlier, their attitudes were rather different. It is said that Luis Figueroa, the Communist union leader, had approached a Santiago businessman, with whom he had remained on friendly terms, and asked him to look after his family if he was forced to leave the country suddenly. That prospect no longer seemed imminent.

But Allende was not persuaded by the wild talk of an 'October revolution'. That would certainly have resulted in a bloody civil war in which his partisans might have proved considerably less strong than the ultras believed. That industrial workers stayed in their factories did not prove that their allegiance to the government was rock-hard; in many cases, they were frightened of being fired by their official managers or *interventores* if they downed tools. The capacity of assault-squads from the *cordones* to break down shop shutters or occupy empty factories, similarly, did not mean that 'revolutionary soviets' were already functioning; this was the first time that the ultras had been able to mobilise a significant number of people in the streets, and they were not prepared for any serious test of strength.

Above all, by unleashing his '15,000 or 20,000 workers' Allende would almost certainly have forfeited the support of the armed forces. He could not afford to do that. The great strength of the government throughout the entire 27 days that the strikes lasted was that it was able to count on the military to take charge of the day-to-day work of law enforcement and even to execute decrees that were highly unpopular—such as the imposition of censorship over the radio stations. It was the continuing loyalty of the armed forces to the elected government and the constitution that Allende decided to build on. His key advisers and intermediaries, as when he had attempted to bring the military into the cabinet at the end of May, were the Communists.

On 2 November, after a prolonged cabinet crisis (during which the opposition parties moved to impeach four ministers) Allende announced a new ministerial team. General Carlos Prats Gonzalez, the army commander-in-chief, was made minister of the interior, while retaining his army post. Air-Force General Claudio Sepulveda became minister of mines, and Admiral Ismael Huerta was made minister of public works. Allende's original intention is said to have been to bring the commanders-in-chief of all three services into the cabinet; but the navy and air-force commanders declined. The military found themselves in curious company. Two other new faces in the cabinet were those of Luis Figueroa, the Communist trade union boss who now combined his old job with that of labour minister, and Rolandó Calderón, a 29 year old Socialist left-winger who had served his political apprenticeship as a peasant organiser and was said to have worked closely with the MIR. Calderón became minister of agriculture, replacing Chonchol, who was one of the ministers who had been threatened with impeachment.

The strike movement had already begun to falter, and General Prats was able to negotiate a rapid settlement with its leaders. The main elements in the compromise agreement that was concluded on 5 November were pledges by the government to suspend takeover moves against the road transport sector and the wholesale trade; to set up a special commission to inquire into complaints from all sectors of private business; and to curb 'foreign extremists' in Chile. General

Prats also promised that there would be no sanctions against those who had participated in the strike, although it later proved difficult to dislodge the militant groups that had ensconced themselves in some factories or to prevent a partial purge of state employees (especially in the Central Bank) who had stopped work during October.

It was perhaps a reflection of Chile's pacific social traditions that a strike movement on this scale had not resulted in widespread violence and scores of deaths, as might well have been the case in many neighbouring countries. The fighting was limited to skirmishes between right-wing youth and left-wing extremists and a series of sabotage attempts against the major roads and railways leading south. But the October strikes did serve to harden the political battle-lines in Chile. As a test of strength between government and opposition, the strike movement was indecisive. It showed that the divided forces of the opposition could move together, but not that they were ready to submit themselves to a central direction. It showed that the Chilean middle class, when hard pressed, was prepared to adopt the traditional tactic of the working class—the general strike—but not that it could use this weapon successfully enough to force the government to change course.

On the other side, the political commission of the MAPU later commented (in an internal party document) that the actions of organised workers from the industrial *cordones* against those who took part in the strike demonstrated their 'enormous revolutionary potential':

> The masses exhibited a degree of initiative, decisiveness, discipline and organic capacity [sic] never before seen in the country. This popular power of the organised, disciplined masses is springing up everywhere and prevents the total paralysation of the economy . . .[19]

That is clearly an exaggeration, but it is certainly true that the extremist organisations in the *cordones* were given a new impetus in the course of the October strike. And it is difficult to find fault with the MAPU analysts when they add that the other great lesson of the strikes was that, for a variety of reasons, the armed forces could not be expected to respond as opposition leaders might have hoped. The armed forces not only saved the country from a violent confrontation in October; they also rescued Allende from the worst political crisis he had had to face. Their new role in the 'civil–military cabinet' did not please the ultras in Popular Unity, who saw it as 'a new triumph for the centrist line' within the government.[20] It did not please many opposition leaders either, since they feared that the military were now in danger of forsaking their tradition of political neutrality and becoming compromised with a Marxist government. The changed political situation compelled the opposition to concentrate almost exclusively on electioneering over the period up to the March 1973 election. Any attempt to return to strike tactics might have meant confronting the armed forces as well as the Allende government, and the combination would have clearly been insuperable.

Notes to this chapter are on page 213

CHAPTER SEVEN

Allende Looks to the Barracks

How was Allende able to create the strange alliance of Marxists and military that ruled Chile after November 1972? The answer partly lies in the genuine desire of the high command to head off the violent confrontation that might have followed in the wake of the October strikes, and to ensure peaceful elections in March 1973. That the military were prepared to take office in Allende's government rather than force his resignation reflected both on the 'constitutionalist' leanings of most senior army officers and the consciousness in all three services that, in a country as complex and highly politicised as Chile, direct intervention against an elected government would be widely resented. Further, a certain sympathy for the original reformist goals of the Popular Unity coalition—though not for Marxism—existed amongst some of the key generals, although not amongst senior naval or airforce officers. These were men, after all, who felt (not without justification) that they had been neglected by previous governments, and denied both social status and adequate rewards for service. Before Allende came to power, it was a rare thing to see a senior officer in uniform in a good restaurant or hotel in Santiago. After the military joined the cabinet, it became commonplace.

The new role of the Chilean military has to be understood in the broader Latin-American context. No one today would be tempted to describe the armed forces of Latin America as 'the watchdogs of the ruling classes'. Radical generals in Peru, Bolivia (until Colonel Banzer's counter-coup) and more re-

L

cently in Panama have attacked the role of foreign investors
and the United States and promoted a more equitable distribution of wealth within their countries. By a curious mirror-
effect, some of the most hard-nosed guerrilla hunters—those
who broke the back of the Peruvian MIR or the Uruguayan
Tupamaro movement—ended up espousing some of the ideas
of the revolutionaries they had fought. Nor were radical military regimes a phenomenon peculiar to the 1960s and 1970s.
Populist soldiers such as Perón in Argentina, General Rojas
Pinilla in Colombia, General Lázaro Cardenas in Mexico or
Carlos Ibáñez in Chile had transformed the social life of
their countries.[1]

More recently, the radicalism of military establishments
in Latin America has resulted less from the charisma of individual soldier-politicians than from the influence of novel
conceptions of security and development taught by the senior
military colleges. The idea has taken root that the military
must have a hand in national development and that they are
particularly well-equipped (both because of specialised training in engineering, medicine and so on and because in countries with poorly-developed political institutions, they may
appear the only truly national organisation) to do so. That
idea is differently interpreted by the Escola Superior de
Guerra in Brazil and the Centro de Altos Estudios Militares
in Peru, but it has achieved a general currency—welcome,
no doubt, to peacetime soldiers searching for a meaningful
role in society. It was an idea that had been taken up in the
Chilean training establishments also, and could be used to
provide a kind of justification for military participation in a
Marxist-controlled administration, first as technical functionaries, and finally at cabinet level. But it was still clear that,
by drawing the armed forces into politics, Allende was break-
ing with national tradition and setting a dangerous precedent.
In order to ensure his short-term survival, he completely
changed the rules of the country's political game. After
November 1972, it ceased to be inconceivable that the country would eventually be ruled by a military president.

Allende's *autogolpe* (or 'self-made coup') not only disconcerted his opponents, but divided his supporters. The MIR, predictably, saw the formation of the new cabinet as a setback for the revolution. The *mirista* organ, *El Rebelde,* declared in an editorial that the October strikes had presented the 'masses' with the chance to assume total power; but instead, 'the reformists in the government preferred to ally themselves with the high command'.[2] The left wing of the Socialist Party took the same view. One of the publications of the extremist 'eleno' group—published in the premises of the government newspaper, *La Nación*—complained that Allende seemed to have forgotten that 'it was the physical presence of millions of workers that saved the government in October'.[3]

Carlos Altamirano, the Socialist Party's secretary-general was privately bitterly opposed to the inclusion of the military in the cabinet, as was Rolandó Calderón, the new agriculture minister. But Altamirano confined his public criticisms to an attack on the deal that brought an end to the strikes on 5 November. He called for a purge of all state employees who had stopped work. Altamirano and the new economy minister, Fernando Flores (a MAPU member who introduced rationing to postwar Chile) were both of the opinion that—whatever General Prats had promised—none of the enterprises that had been intervened or forcibly taken over during the strikes should be restored to their owners.

It was the Christian Left, curiously enough, that carried its opposition to the new cabinet to the point of dropping out of the government altogether. The party's official statement explained that, despite Chonchol's resignation from the ministry of agriculture, the Christian Left would remain a member of the Popular Unity alliance. The party demanded that the opposition groups that had organised the October strikes should be proscribed[4]—a further example of how those who had once shared the Christian Democrats' hopes of a non-Marxist 'third way' had now cast their lot with the exponents of class war and the dictatorship of the proletariat.

In contrast, the Communists openly welcomed the 'nondeliberative' support of the military. In a statement put out by the party's political commission, they commented that 'the new cabinet will assure the continuity of the revolutionary process... The presence of the armed forces is a patriotic necessity at this moment.'[5] The continuing conflict between the two Marxist parties within Allende's government thus assumed a new character: while the Socialists and the Catholic left drew closer to the revolutionary groups that had boycotted the elections and the whole constitutional process, the Communists looked for allies among the men in uniform.

The novelty of what the Chilean press soon took to calling the 'civilian–military cabinet' should not be exaggerated. Historians might find precedents in the 1920s and 1930s. In 1924, for example, President Arturo Alessandri, locked in a conflict with Congress, tried to intimidate his parliamentary opponents by bringing military men into his cabinet, with General Altamirano Talavera as his minister of interior. He got his reformist labour laws through Congress, but General Altamirano rapidly developed an appetite for power, closed down parliament altogether, and set up a military junta with himself at the head. It took a counter-coup by a group of radical younger officers (including Colonel Marmaduque Grove) to bring Alessandri back early in 1925.

For a second time, Alessandri was unfortunate in his choice of a military minister. He was shown the door by his new minister of war, Colonel Carlos Ibáñez, who installed a straw man in his place and finally (in 1927) used his strategic new appointment as minister of the interior to make himself president. Ibáñez fell after four years of comparatively prosperous authoritarian rule (not dictatorial, since he did not do away with Congress and the constitution) leaving the country in the throes of the Great Depression. The last successful intervention of the military in Chilean politics came in 1932, when Marmaduque Grove led a conspiracy that set up the short-lived 'Socialist Republic' to which the Allende government owed many of its most useful legal powers.[6]

These isolated cases of military intervention in Chilean

politics did not result in any prolonged experiment in military government. The most celebrated of all—the overthrow of the reformist President Balmaceda by the navy and a section of the army in 1891 when he attempted to ride roughshod over Congress—was also one of the clearest examples of the military confining its role to that of the final arbiter, stepping in to clear the decks and then withdrawing from the fray. Since 1932, there were a series of military conspiracies, leading up to General Roberto Viaux's 'Tacnazo' in 1969. But none of them came close to success. It was Allende's singular distinction to have brought the military back into Chilean politics.

It is worth examining the process by which a Marxist government was able to co-opt the high command. One thing in Allende's favour was that the Chilean officer corps did not match any prefabricated model of a conservative military elite. A RAND Corporation survey carried out in the mid-1960s showed that the attitudes of Chilean officers, and their social backgrounds, were comparable to those of any other branch of the public service. An overwhelming majority of those interviewed declared that they supported the existing constitution. Only 2.8 per cent of the senior officers interviewed were classified as right wing, while more than a quarter were classified as left wing.[7]

The RAND survey also showed that, since 1945, the Chilean army had evolved into a highly professional force, drawing most of its officers from the lower middle class or from civil service or military families. About a third of the generals and colonels interviewed (on both the active and retired lists) said that they had enlisted in order to make more money and achieve higher living standards than their parents had enjoyed. The social origins of army officers cannot, of course, be taken as a reliable gauge of their likely political leanings. The class breakdown of the Brazilian and Peruvian officer corps reveals a broadly similar pattern[8]—and yet it is hard to think of two military regimes that have adopted such diverse political strategies.

From the outset, Allende's survival depended on how he dealt with the armed forces. Although the circumstances surrounding the Schneider killing showed that a number of senior officers were deeply hostile to Allende (see Chapter 2) the attitudes of the officer corps in general were rather more ambiguous. Allende was able, for instance, to profit from the widespread resentment inspired by low wages, declining social status, and what many officers felt to be the 'neglect' shown by successive governments. There were stirrings in the barracks as early as April 1968, when army demands for a pay increase forced Frei to replace his defence minister and his commander-in-chief. But the Christian Democrats failed to produce the goods. In October 1969, Viaux (at that time the commander of the Antofagasta garrison) sent a strongly-worded letter to the president protesting at low wage levels and continuing governmental neglect. Frei's answer was to fire him, which led to the revolt of the Tacna armoured regiment in sympathy with him, and Chile was treated to the unfamiliar spectacle of tanks and armoured personnel carriers converging on the presidential palace. The Tacnazo soon fizzled out (some of the tanks were so antiquated that they failed to start up) but Allende took great care after he assumed office to remove the conditions that had led to it.

As part of his first *reajuste* (or raise in salaries) he substantially increased soldiers' pay, uniform allowances and family benefits. He also expanded the budget for defence equipment. Even when the government had exhausted its foreign reserves and was forced to impose tight exchange controls, the navy and the air force had little difficulty in getting the budget allocations to buy new equipment in Europe.

Allende was also able to profit from a certain personal *entrée* to the officer corps as a Freemason and a Socialist. Nearly a fifth of the Chilean army officers are said to be masons, including General Prats, Allende's loyal servant. The Socialist Party's influence dates from its very foundation in 1933, when Marmaduque Grove, formerly the air-force commander, became its first leader. It is worth noting that

Frei was so alarmed by the unauthorised contacts between Allende and the then naval chief, Admiral Porta Angulo, that he sacked him and appointed a conservative officer, Admiral Hugo Tirado, in his place.[9] After November 1970, Allende's skilful courtship of the men in uniform was the most striking example of his gifts as a politician. He missed very few opportunities to review a parade or pin on a medal. The joke circulated that the president's latest mistress was Marina (the Navy). He presented one of his generals with a huge inscribed silver cigarette-case on the first anniversary of his appointment to office; another with a silver replica of the sword of the national hero, Bernardo O'Higgins.

At first, Allende avoided open interference with the chain of command and discouraged attempts at subversion within the barracks by his Marxist supporters—although a concerted, and partially successful, attempt was made to politicise the anti-riot units of the paramilitary police, or Carabineros. He may have remembered that what finally persuaded the Brazilian generals to move against Goulart in 1964, after more than two years of economic chaos, high inflation, and the organisation of paramilitary groups on the far left, was a threat to the internal discipline of the armed forces. At any rate, Allende began his term by passing up the golden opportunity presented to him by Schneider's death to pack the army high command with his own nominees. The Chilean army's system of seniority is as constricting as a whalebone corset. When a new commanding officer is appointed, all serving officers senior to him must resign their commissions. By appointing a youngish, left-leaning officer, Allende could thus have shown most of his generals the door. Instead, he chose Prats, already the next in line. And instead of giving the ministry of defence to a Marxist who might have aroused the army's suspicions, he gave it to a Radical (Alejandro Rios) already well-known to the military because of his many years as an instructor at the Escuela Militar. (Later, the defence ministry was transferred to a 'moderate' Socialist, José Tohá.)

Allende's careful neutrality in handling the armed forces

did not last indefinitely. During his first two years, there were
two notable cases of political sackings. The first involved
Colonel Alberto Labbé, the commandant of the Santiago military academy. Labbé was an outspoken conservative who was
vehemently opposed to Castro's trip to Chile in 1971 and fell
under government suspicion when most of his cadets fell
victim to a mysterious influenza epidemic on the eve of the
Cuban leader's scheduled visit to the college. Labbé was
demoted to a desk job, and then made to resign. He later
ran as a National Party candidate in the senate elections in
Santiago in March 1973, when he was narrowly defeated.

The second, and much more controversial case, involved
General Alfredo Canales Marquez, the army director of training. He was called into retirement in September 1972, after
a naval colleague, Admiral Justiniano, had reported some
remarks he had made criticising the government's economic
policies. After his forced retirement, Canales expressed himself frankly in a series of press interviews. He drew attention
to the proliferation of paramilitary groups on the extreme
left and criticised those of his colleagues who believed that
no action should be taken against them until they had com-
pleted their 'preparatory phase' (recruitment, indoctrination,
acquisition of arms and supplies) and embarked on full-
scale guerrilla operations. 'Paramilitary forces,' he declared,
'should not exist within a country, and since, in the long
term, their aim is to destroy the army, it is the duty of the
armed forces to be alive to the threat.'[10]

Canales argued that the 'duty' of the armed forces should
extend to pressuring the government into taking firmer measures against armed extremists and passing whatever new
laws might be necessary. Normally, he maintained, the army's
views should be expressed through the normal channels—ie,
from the high command to the president's National Security
Council. He warned of 'a loss of discipline and cohesion' if
a commander-in-chief 'failed to represent the army's feelings
effectively'.[11] Canales also attacked the Marxists' conception
of class struggle and appealed for a return to nationalism.[12]

But Canales' most interesting comments involved the so-called 'Schneider doctrine'—the views on the role of the armed forces that were most fully expressed by the former commander-in-chief in a letter to *El Mercurio* before the 1970 election. Schneider had insisted that the army must remain studiously neutral in political terms, confining its role to the defence of national sovereignty and the constitution.[13] To Canales, it seemed that the 'Schneider doctrine' had to be reinterpreted in conditions where a country seemed to be teetering to the brink of civil war:

I have always leaned towards this view of the Schneider doctrine, that as a government loses its grip in a particular country, the armed forces must correspondingly adopt a firmer position in order to make it deal with the problems. From this, one can arrive at obvious conclusions. The armed forces have the moral responsibility to avoid civil conflict and civil war ... I do not believe and I refuse to believe that the armed forces are going to allow a million people to die in this country before they do something ... The armed forces have the responsibility, acting in collaboration with the government, to prevent the killing of a single Chilean.[14]

It is interesting to compare Canales' views with the theory of 'co-participation' espoused by General Prats when the military agreed to enter the cabinet in November 1972.

The formation of a Marxist–military government was the culmination of the gradual process by which Allende had transferred more and more administrative authority to members of the high command in order to give them a vested interest in the new order. General Pedro Palacios, an army engineer, served as Allende's minister of mines until the June 1972 cabinet reshuffle. (He was brought in to replace the Radical politician, Orlando Cantuarias after evidence of shady dealings by government officials had come to light.) After his resignation, he was given a fairly insignificant job as chief of recruitment—which some officers regarded as punishment for his previous involvement with the regime.

Below cabinet level, the military were given an important role to play in the state corporations, and during the first two years of the Popular Unity government, senior officers (on both the active and the retired lists) were appointed to the boards of some forty state enterprises and research institutions —including CORFO, the Nuclear Energy Commission and the management of the mines. General Orlando Urbina, commander of the Second Division, had the responsibility of organising the UNCTAD III conference in Santiago in April 1972. Senior officers were also sometimes used as *interventores* in conflict situations, although this was resisted by the extreme left.

Allende's policy of co-opting the armed forces was in fact highly controversial within the ranks of the Popular Unity coalition, as the varying reactions to the creation of the joint cabinet demonstrated. Many of the left-wingers within Allende's own party subscribed to the views of Raul Ampuero, a former Socialist secretary-general who had set up a small splinter party (USOPO). In an important speech delivered in Concepción in August 1971, Ampuero had insisted on the need for two basic changes in the organisation of the Chilean armed forces. The first would be 'a substantial change in the command' to ensure that the security forces would be 'formally subordinated to the same political direction that is guiding the struggle for socialism and independence'. This would mean both a purge of political 'doubtfuls' within the high command, and the appointment of political commissars. Secondly, Ampuero called for a system of 'total people's defence' modelled on North Vietnam and designed to counter an internal political threat—'the substitution of a reactionary regime in bondage to foreign capital for the people's government'. The new system would involve the creation of civilian militias and of citizens' auto-defence groups closely controlled by Popular Unity committees.

To mention the phrase 'popular militia' to a regular soldier in time of peace, of course, is like showing a red rag to a bull. Allende had explicitly promised that no popular militias would be formed during his term of office.[15] But he was never fully in control of the left-wing extremists in the MIR and in the Marxist parties who felt differently. The *miristas*, for instance, attracted a certain number of conscript soldiers to political rallies in the slum *poblaciones* and had detailed plans for infiltrating the command structure (see Chapter 5). They had some initial success in winning over subalterns in the Chilean army's elite 'black berets'.

Even the Communist Party, highly sensitive to the threat of a coup inspired by extremist provocation, spawned some dangerous 'young Turks'. Party documents leaked to *El Mercurio* suggested that the Communist youth movement had its own plans for subverting conscript soldiers. Although senior party spokesmen denied all responsibility for these documents, some were found in the possession of Patricio Cueto Roman, a 23 year old Communist agitator working in the Valparaiso area. One memorandum outlined the following set of 'urgent instructions':

1. Registration of each draftee in his respective canton, since the central committee states that no comrade of draft age for military service shall abstain from doing his term ...
2. Preparation of a general register of comrades who join the service, including the location, regiment and province ... No member may abstain from doing his compulsory military service and the committee must be informed of any member who has not registered or presented himself at the appointed date.
3. The comrades must be indoctrinated before joining the service so that they will be aware of their role during this period.[16]

This document was unsettling, early evidence of a Communist attempt at subversion within the barracks aimed to produce a disciplined core of party members within the ranks of the conscripts. It is pretty flimsy evidence to go on, but it may suggest that the Communist leaders were contemplating from quite early on their own version of the Socialists' *doble militancia*: a dual strategy designed to win the support or neutrality of the armed forces (and the middle class) while also creating the framework for a 'people's army' at the service of the party in the event of civil war or a bid for total power.

In the short term, however, it was the first part of that strategy that paid dividends. It is reliably reported that at the end of May 1972, Allende followed the Communists' advice by offering no fewer than five cabinet seats to the military—although he never publicly admitted that the offer had been made. Their agreement to join the government six months later saved Allende from the consequences of one of the worst social and economic crises that Chile had had to face since 1945. It also raised the question of whether the generals could really remain politically neutral if they accepted key positions within a Marxist-controlled government. Every move that the military made over the four months between their admission to the cabinet and the March 1973 elections was dissected in the Santiago salons as a clue to whether the armed forces were content merely to underwrite the government's programme or whether they were ready to steer it in a new direction. The debate increasingly centred on the personality of one man: General Carlos Prats Gonzalez.

Prats was still very much an unknown quantity to the Chilean public when he arrived in the ministry of the interior. At fifty-seven, he had spent nearly all of his working life in Chile since he had been commissioned as a gunnery lieutenant in 1934, apart from a short term as military attaché in Buenos Aires, where he came to know many of the senior officers in the Argentine army. His pastimes were not of a purely military bent; he was a competent painter and essayist (mainly on military history) as well as a good horseman. He had known Schneider, his predecessor as commander-in-chief, since he had been a captain, and shared some of Schneider's

views on the non-political character of the armed forces and
their duty to contribute to social and economic development.
Interviewed on television just after he joined the cabinet,
Prats insisted that it was not a 'co-government' of soldiers and
politicians because that term implied that each group had
separate policies. 'What we have is co-participation of political
parties and the armed forces. The cabinet is a working body
that acts according to the direct instructions of the President
of the Republic.'[17]

It is doubtful whether General Prats's definition of the role
of the Chilean cabinet, and the functions of the military
ministers within it, would find favour with many constitutional lawyers. He based himself on Article 22 of the Chilean
constitution, which rules that the armed forces are to obey,
not to take decisions (*obediente y no deliberante*). But once
the military had joined the cabinet, they were inevitably
drawn into the rough-and-tumble of party politics. And when
Allende left the country for a fortnight in December to visit
Russia, Cuba and the United Nations, Prats became vice-
president and acting head of state. Was it really possible to
make out that the commander-in-chief was still *obediente y
no deliberante*?

General Prats told the left-wing weekly, *Chile Hoy*, that he
saw two main tasks before the new government: to restore
social peace, and to clear the way for honest, unviolent elections in March. It had some more immediate obligations. The
government had broadcast an important declaration on 5
November that brought an end to the strikes. One of its
most important clauses stipulated that there would be 'no
reprisals' against those who had taken part in strike action.
This implied that property that had been requisitioned or
illegally seized by workers and left-wing extremists in October would be returned to its owners and that employees of
state enterprises who had stopped work would not be dis-
criminated against. In the months that followed, some of the
160-odd businesses that had been seized were returned to their
proprietors, despite bitter resistance by the *miristas*. In Arica,

miristas who had occupied electronics firms and locked out the 1,800 workers who had joined the strike were evicted on General Prats's orders; it was notable that under the new government the police moved much more quickly to enforce court orders restoring intervened property to its owners.

But the military did not prevent the purge of anti-government employees in some state enterprises. While medical staff who had been sacked by hospitals in Los Angeles and Curico were reinstated, more than seventy employees of the state railways were dismissed, together with twenty-eight employees of the Central Bank, which had become a Communist Party stronghold.

Nor did the presence of the military in the government serve to check the rising violence in the country. The death of a young National Party member, Hector Castillo, when student groups clashed during a university election at Chillán late in December, led to an acid exchange in the senate between Prats and Senator Alfredo Lorca, a Christian Democrat. Lorca asked why the Carabineros were not present at the meeting, and why they did not intervene to prevent the bloodshed. Prats replied that he regarded university meetings as peaceful occasions. When Lorca remarked that 'he must be living in some other country', Prats lost his temper and declared that he would not tolerate an insult to his uniform. Lorca pointed out that he appeared in the chamber in his capacity as minister, not as a general. The squabble ended with each man charging the other with insolence.

The incident, trivial in itself, showed up the contradictions in General Prats's effort to present himself as a non-political minister. The killing that gave rise to it demonstrated one of the problems that Prats and his colleagues had inherited: the presence of radical Marxists in the middle echelons of the administration. The man who was really to blame for the non-intervention of the Carabineros at Chillán was the *intendente* of Nuble province, a MAPU militant called Luis Quezada who had left no one in doubt of his neutrality when he declared, on being appointed, that he would not be the governor of all the province, but of the workers alone. He took no action while armed bands of Socialist militants roamed the main square of Chillán prior to the shootings.

Another firebrand among the *intendentes* was Jaime Faivovich, the Socialist who was made governor of Santiago at the end of 1972.[18] A long-time Socialist, he had briefly figured as the party's secretary-general before the 1958 elections. He later became prominent within the left-wing faction that pressed for closer links with the extra-parliamentary groups such as the MIR, and continued to serve on the editorial board of *Punto Final* after he was given his Santiago job. Middle-class residents of the capital were not reassured to learn that during the 1970 election campaign, Faivovich had suggested that the Popular Unity alliance should include 'revolutionary tribunals and firing squads' in its programme. He was said to have told the slum settlers of Lo Hermida 'to go into the courts and slaughter those miserable old mummies'. Even more disturbing than Faivovich's appointment was the confirmation of his predecessor, Alfredo Joignant (who had once threatened to invade the middle-class *barrio alto* with 40,000 workers) as chief of *Investigaciones*, the Chilean CID.

With men like Faivovich and Quezada working to overthrow 'bourgeois legality' at a lower level, the military ministers found themselves in a very difficult position. The Communists, still feuding with the Socialist left, might have been willing to back them in a partial purge of the would-be guerrillas within the administration; but that might have led to a complete rift in the government on the eve of a vital election. General Prats at least preferred to present himself as holding the ring for the March elections. This meant applying the brakes to the government programme rather than trying to swing it back the other way. The military ministers could at least take credit for a number of measures that helped to safeguard the freedom of the media during the run-up to the elections. The most important was the belated concessions of fair prices for the products of the *Papelera*. Radio Agricultura de los Angeles (closed during the strikes) was allowed to reopen. Two southern newspapers (*El Sur* and *La Mañana*) that had been seized by left-wing extremists were restored to their proprietors.

It is too early to write the full story of what took place in the cabinet meetings after the military joined the government. The military found themselves in an awkward position. One of the initial fears of the opposition was that, as career soldiers without training in economics or political debate, the military ministers would be outfoxed by practised dialecticians like the Communist finance minister, Orlando Millas, and persuaded to acquiesce in divisive policies. In fact, at least one of the military ministers, Admiral Ismael Huerta, took care to keep himself properly briefed by asking for regular reports on the state of the economy from experts from outside government circles. The military ministers did not have formal responsibility for the domestic economy, but they were bound to be wary of letting themselves become too closely identified with the mistakes of the government planners. They were not willing, as it turned out, to sign 'decrees of insistence' to enable the government to override court rulings in order to take over firms.

But it seems that they were not even consulted on the system of rationing adopted by the government in January 1973. The extremely partisan speech in which the new finance minister, Fernando Flores, announced the new system was appropriately summarised in a cartoon-commentary in the left-wing paper *Ultima Hora* in which Flores was shown boasting that the poor would eat well and the rich would eat shit. In two strongly-worded letters to the president of *El Mercurio*,[19] Allende subsequently argued that the new system could not be described as rationing, because ration cards were not going to be introduced. That seemed a curious argument to many Chileans, since rationing cards had not even been used during the two world wars or the depression, while the Communists and left-wing extremists who controlled most of the local 'committees of prices and supply' (known as JAPs)

had been issuing their own ration cards in workers' suburbs.
I was shown one of these cards, stamped with the slogan: 'this
card comes from the masses'. Call it what you will, the Flores
scheme in its original form seemed to give the Communist-
dominated JAPs alarming powers to organise and supervise
the lives of local communities. Under the new system, each
family was to claim its regular quota of basic foodstuffs, like
rice, coffee, oil, milk, meat and sugar, which would be put
on sale at fixed prices. The catch was that the JAPs would
determine 'the real needs' of each family. As Flores put it,

> The JAPs will take the necessary measures to create a stable
> relationship between families and shopkeepers in each area.
> To do this, it is essential to know the real necessities of
> each family and each shopkeeper in a particular area.
> Therefore, the JAPs will define the real needs of each
> family.[20]

In other words, the Communists' neighbourhood cells were
to be licensed to enter private houses and pry into the larder
and to practise intimidation by threatening to cut off food
supplies. It was not just a system that was open to political
abuse; it was a recipe for political control through the
stomach, and ex-president Frei denounced it as 'a clear and
definitive move towards totalitarian control in this country'.
Banner-headlines in the opposition press echoed his judge-
ment: 'The shadow of dictatorship' (*El Mercurio*); 'Rationing: Popular Unity's death-blow to Chile' (*Las Ultimas
Noticias*); 'Chile says NO: National repudiation of rationing'
(*La Prensa*).

Admiral Ismael Huerta first learned the news of the new
rationing measures when he opened his newspaper on Friday
morning. He immediately telephoned to Prats and General
Claudio Sepulveda and arranged a meeting for 10 o'clock that
morning. None of them admitted to having received prior
warning of the Flores speech, although later Prats privately
informed friends that he had been told in advance. That

M

afternoon, they met with Allende, who stalled for time by insisting that the military were in the cabinet 'not as individuals, but as the representatives of institutions', and that their decisions would have to be discussed in a fuller meeting with the commanders of the navy and the air force as well. This was arranged for the following Monday. Over the weekend, the military ministers met again around a Santiago swimming-pool and appeared still to be agreed on their decision to resign. Admiral Huerta was assured of the full support of the navy in maintaining his stand.

But the following week, in a new series of talks with Allende, Prats seemed more disposed to bargain. Allende is said to have repeatedly appealed to the military to show their gratitude 'for all I have done for you—and especially for you, Admiral'. José Tohá, who joined in one of the meetings, is said to have warned that if they left the government, the country might face a left-wing insurrection. Allende was unable to conceal his alarm about the political consequences of the resignation of the military ministers on the eve of the election. At one stage, he is said to have stormed up and down his room in La Moneda and shouted at Prats and Huerta that, if abandoned by the armed forces he would not seek refuge in Cuba. 'I will take refuge in the Cordón de Cerillos' (one of Santiago's industrial areas), he is supposed to have said, 'and they will never throw me out of there.' As if to prove his point, he disappeared into the *cordón* two days before Admiral Huerta resigned his portfolio and spent his time haranguing workers in the nationalised textile firms on such timely subjects as the dangers of alcoholism in Chile.

A week passed, and Prats spent part of the following weekend talking with Huerta and Admiral Montero in Viña del Mar, that beautiful resort-town of retired sailors and sunbathers. The outline of a compromise agreement had now been worked out. The military would present a list of eight points to be settled by Allende. Their key demands included: control of the economy by a military man, as either minister of finance or minister of economy; a tight rein of the JAPs;

military control of the overall process of food distribution;
and an assurance that in future, left-wing provincial governors would permit the police to execute court orders. If
Allende was prepared to concede a reasonable proportion of
these demands, the military would remain in the cabinet, but
Huerta (now totally disenchanted with his role in the
'Marxist experiment') would be allowed to resign and hand
over to another admiral. As it transpired, Allende was prepared to give the military partial satisfaction on every point,
except for their demand for one of the economic ministries.
Admiral Huerta dropped out of the cabinet but kept his rank
as vice-admiral and took over responsibility for naval pro-
curement (a far from insignificant job at a moment when the
Russians were offering considerable military aid). Admiral
Arellano—once privately described by Prats, as Santiago
rumour has it, as 'my only friend who is an admiral'—was
appointed as Huerta's successor.

As part of his new deal with the military, Allende appointed the chief accountant to the air force, General Alberto
Bachelet, to run a new state distribution authority, the
National Secretariat of Distribution and Commercialisation.
Bachelet had held other technical jobs in the administration
and, as a relative of the Radical Senator, Hugo Miranda, was
regarded as not unsympathetic to Allende's programme. But
his new job proved to be singularly frustrating, and the
clashes between Bachelet's staff and the left-wing extremists
soon appeared to be leading towards a new show-down between the government and the military. Bachelet's appointment was designed to reassure the public that the JAPs would
not be allowed a free hand to practise the more sinister kind
of political control—control through the stomachs. But its
effect was clearly meant to be cosmetic rather than real.
Bachelet's staff consisted of only three army colonels and a
naval captain, Parodi, who fanned out to inquire into the
affairs of the four state distributing companies.

It was not long before their role was directly challenged by
the extreme left. On 22 February, only ten days before the

election, the offices of the nationalised distribution company, Agencias Graham, were occupied by a band of *miristas* led by two young hotheads from the 'Lo Hermida' settlement who called themselves 'Comandante Raul' and 'Comandante Micky'. Agencias Graham came under the supervision of Captain Parodi, who—in accordance with Bachelet's instructions—had acted a few days earlier to remove a militant manager who had been agitating for more 'workers' control' over rationing and production. Now the *miristas*, without police or army interference, threw out his successor, Julio Stuardo, and appointed another extremist, Sergio Juárez, in his place. The *miristas*, encamped in the company offices, proceeded to issue fiery communiqués in which they called for expropriation of all large wholesalers and retailers.[21] Allende, frightened of full-scale street-fighting on the eve of the elections, refused to evict the *miristas* and when the military finally left the cabinet a month later, on 27 March, the extremists were still in control of the Agencias Graham. The incident may have appeared marginal in itself, but to many it was an extraordinary example of the powerlessness of the military to impose their wishes on a government in which they participated.

The circumstances under which the military left the government at the end of March are studied in the next chapter. The record of the military during those brief five months of 'co-government' is still ambiguous. The pace of the state takeover of private firms was slowed down, but much of the damage had already been done. The military created the conditions for orderly elections on 4 March, but those elections could not in themselves solve the enormous social and economic problems that Allende's policy had created. The military themselves often seemed confused and divided about their role. While Huerta (and some of his naval colleagues) wanted nothing so much as to wash their hands of the government, General Prats was ready to say on television shortly before the elections that the country was divided between 'progressives, centrists and reactionaries'—

a way of summing things up that dismayed the leaders of the opposition parties but earned him an encomium in the leader pages of *El Siglo*.[22] The rumour circulated that he had been 'bought' by the Communist Party, which—it was alleged —had offered to back him as the presidential candidate of the Popular Unity coalition in the 1976 elections. The rumour may have been false, but it alarmed some opposition politicians. All that was clear was that neither the government nor the opposition could count on the armed forces as an automatic ally.

Notes to this chapter are on page 214

CHAPTER EIGHT

'The People: 43%.
The Reactionaries: 55%.'

Perhaps Chile is the only country in the world where people do not talk as if 51 per cent of the votes is a majority. On the pleasantly sunny morning of Tuesday, 6 March 1973, the pro-Communist Santiago daily, *Puro Chile,* carried the news of a famous victory. Its banner headline proclaimed: 'El Pueblo: 43%. Los Momios: 54·7%.' *Momio* is a remarkable word (it literally means an Egyptian-style mummy) coined by some wit on the Chilean left to describe local reactionaries; now the 'reactionaries', from exiled landowners down to pro-Christian Democrat washerwomen, use it cheerfully to describe themselves. From the results of the congressional elections that had been held on Sunday, 4 March, it thus appeared that Chile was still a country where the *momios* were in a majority. Yet only the left showed any signs of triumph when the final results came out.

Nobody but the Communists expected that the government's supporters would be able to haul in more than 40 per cent of the votes. Shortly before the election, Allende himself was declaring that the important thing was to get more than 36 per cent, his share of the votes in the 1970 presidential election. Opposition leaders, for their part, had been talking wildly about the chance of winning two-thirds of the seats in Congress, which would have given them the power to initiate legislation and impeach the president. That target might have been within reach; the opposition was only two seats away from a two-thirds majority in the Senate and even though only half of the 50 Senate seats were up for election on 4 March, a modest swing might have given CODE what it needed. But on the eve of the election, Eduardo Frei was sensibly urging his supporters to remember that a simple majority for the opposition would serve notice on the government that the country as a whole rejected a programme that was radically transforming its social structures and institutions.

Amateur opinion pollsters popped up on all sides during the months before the election; one American estimate gave the government about 38 per cent; a Socialist Party public opinion survey, carried out back in December, came up with similar results, showing a rout for the Popular Unity candidates in Santiago; military intelligence reports showed a particularly strong swing to the opposition parties in the coastal towns, and gave CODE some 72 per cent of the votes in Valparaiso. These various opinion polls and voting surveys now have a purely historical interest, but it is worth noting, for the record, that the Communist Party (which never conducts opinion polls but simply goes by the estimates of its local cadres) was the only body that predicted the results accurately. The same was true in earlier elections. At the end of February, the Communists expected Popular Unity to draw 42 per cent of the votes.

It was not a typical Chilean election. Far too much was at stake. While Carlos Altamirano was ready to shrug off the election as 'a routine democratic exercise', Allende was fully aware that in some sense it was a pebiscite. Even if the opposition failed to get two-thirds of the votes, a major swing away from the government would be bound to make the military reconsider their position within the government and would explode its claim to be a 'people's government'. This was partly why the election campaign was distinguished by a torrent of personal abuse and rumour-mongering without parallel in recent Chilean history. The left-wing daily, *Clarín*, distinguished itself by publishing trick photographs in which the National Party leader, Sr Sergio Onofre Jarpa, was depicted as a naked whore with a swastika around his neck. This kind of public-lavatory humour was less sinister than the new campaign to destroy the image of ex-president Frei, which resulted in a series of poisonous articles in *Puro Chile* representing him as 'Mister Frei,' the creature of Washington.

Despite the build-up of tension during the huge street-rallies over the week before polling day, and the minor clashes during smaller *concentraciones* in working-class areas (when left-wing militants tried to prevent Jarpa and the National Party youth leader, Juan Luis Ossa, from entering their chosen territory) Sunday passed off smoothly. The soldiers were thick on the ground and carried out their promise to maintain order. The dark rumours that the MIR was planning to invade the centre of Santiago with armed workers from the *cordones* in the event of a rout for the government came to nothing, although there were some minor incidents that night. Around 11 pm, just before Allende made his first statement on the incoming election results, armed *miristas* in a truck ran down a motorcycle policeman who tried to flag them down. After midnight, as reports of extremist concentrations in the Avenida Kennedy began to flow in, the police sealed off the area around Allende's private residence in the Avenida Tomas Moro.

The demonstrations that followed on Monday and Tuesday might have been bigger but for the curious way in which the election results were announced. In every free election in living memory in Chile, the results had been broadcast on the night of the balloting. This time, there was a delay of nearly 24 hours, so that the final figures were not known until Monday evening. This interval helped to defuse some of the tension that built up on Sunday night. But the reasons for this unprecedented delay were not entirely clear. There were 800,000-odd new voters (illiterates and over-18s) to be counted, it was true. But the polling mechanisms proved unusually inefficient.

The votes in a Chilean election are counted, in the first instance, by some 20,000 voting *mesas*. The votes of men and women are counted separately. Each *mesa* is composed of four people chosen by lot from the district electoral register, and supervised by a number of *apoderados*—representatives of the different political parties—who must also be present. Each *mesa* is supposed to stay open for eight hours on voting day, although they are not required to start functioning at any particular time. Once the votes have been collected and counted at this level, the results are sent on to the office of the provincial *intendente* who in turn passes them on to the central electoral office—which was set up this time in the building that had been constructed for the UNCTAD III conference in April 1973. The sealed bags of votes are supposed to be passed on to a committee of scrutineers who will laboriously recheck the count over a period of months to ensure that there has been no fiddling with the figures.

It was clear, as the figures started to flow in on Sunday night, that many of the *mesas* (and above all the women's counting-tables) had been abnormally slow in getting themselves organised. Some of the last results of all to come in were those of women in middle-class residential areas in Santiago, where the vote against the government was overwhelming. This initial skewing of the results frustrated opposition leaders, and some of them became convinced, as they listened to the monotonous, slurring voice of Daniel Vergara, the Communist deputy minister of interior, giving out his periodic *informes*, that someone had been tampering with the results.

There is no doubt that there was some electoral fraud. Bundles of presumably stolen votes—all of them for opposition candidates—were later discovered in Santiago, and children were discovered picking up pilfered ballot papers under the Pedro de Valdivia bridge and taking them home as souvenirs. It was discovered that some *mesas* in remoter rural areas had been improperly constituted, in the absence of accredited opposition representatives. It was suggested that some of the subtotals might have been juggled in the offices of provincial *intendentes*. Later investigations carried out by the law faculty of the Catholic University of Santiago led to charges that up to 5 per cent of the pro-government votes may have been fictitious although these charges received almost no attention in the western newspapers that had reported Allende's electoral 'victory'.

But it must be admitted that Popular Unity made a much stronger showing in the March elections than most observers had thought possible. The advances made by the Marxist parties can give the misleading impression that they gained more ground than they really did, since the real comparison is with the last congressional election in 1969, before Allende took office. By comparison with the most recent nation-wide elections—the municipal elections of April 1971—the Popular Unity vote actually dropped by more than 6 per cent. Even so, the Communists gained another deputy and two more senators, and the Socialists surged forward from 14 to 27 deputies and from 3 to 5 senators. Among the smaller parties in Allende's coalition, only MAPU did well; the Radicals lost more than half of their seats in the lower house, and were clearly finished as a significant political force in Chile. The government coalition as a whole emerged with 63 deputies and 19 senators (against 57 and 16 before); the opposition was left with 87 and 30, compared with 93 and 32 before.

On the other side of the political spectrum, the Nationals did well. Although they failed to get Colonel Alberto Labbé (their second senate candidate in Santiago) elected, they increased their overall share of the vote, and emerged with 21 per cent as the second strongest party in the country, after the Christian Democrats with 29 per cent. The Nationals' gains demonstrated the new strength of the right as a reaction to Dr Allende's policies. The successes of both the Nationals and the Socialists (whose senate candidate in Santiago, Carlos Altamirano, polled more votes than his Communist rival, the supple and diplomatic Volodia Teitelboim) enabled the government paper *La Nación* to argue that 'centrist positions which supposedly interpret the interests of the middle class' had been rejected by both sides. There appeared to be some truth in that, and the shrinking vote for the 'centrists' was probably only to be expected during a period when the political forces in the country were becoming increasingly polarised. But there was no one-way trend. Among the Christian Democrats, for example, the closest supporters of Eduardo Frei (who followed the most consistent anti-Marxist line) did well in the senate election. But in the elections for the lower house, Bernardo Leighton, a veteran party politician who has frequently served as the Christian Democrats' link-man with the Communists, won the biggest personal majority in Santiago's first district.

The question that must be asked is: how did Popular Unity manage to win more than 40 per cent of the votes in March, if Allende's government committed as many mistakes as this book has suggested? The results made it plain, to begin with, that not all Chileans were equally concerned about the state of the economy. Recent official wage increases had been designed to benefit the lowest-paid workers, but not white-collar workers or professional men. Thus the government bought the support of those at the bottom of the social scale, while steadily tightening the vice on other occupational groups. Allende could also count on the backing of those who had been formerly unemployed and had managed to find jobs in state-run industries; it was estimated that the number of people employed by the state had risen by no less than 80 per cent since Allende had taken office, and it has been shown in an earlier chapter that in some private firms the total number of employees had more than doubled since state managers took over. There were other factors in Allende's favour that were less quantifiable. The elections took place in summer, in that pleasant dry heat fanned by the cooling winds from the Pacific, when it was rather less irksome to have to queue for twelve hours to buy a chicken (the experience of ordinary working-class housewives in Lo Hermida) than it would be the following winter. Working-class Chileans had more paper money in their pockets than they had possibly ever dreamed of before, and although it was worth less every time they looked at it, it gave the temporary illusion of affluence. In rural areas (where the government scored relatively better than in the towns), the food shortages were not yet so acute as in Santiago. And there was one final factor that was a little more unsettling than any of the things that have been mentioned. It was the increased control that the government was able to exercise over the daily lives of the residents of working-class districts through neighbourhood committees and the new system of rationing introduced by Sr Flores in January.

No simple class analysis is sufficient to explain the election results. That was brought home to me during a visit to the Lo Hermida *población* shortly before the elections. Lo Hermida, a dusty, depressing shanty-town of wooden shacks lacking some of the basic services, was often cited as a Marxist stronghold among the working-class areas of Santiago. I found the reality rather more complex and troubling, for what was happening in Lo Hermida was an example of how political pluralism was being slowly trampled down by the range of pressures that the Marxist parties can bring to bear on ordinary citizens. Lo Hermida was overshadowed by a *mirista* encampment, the hang-out of 'Comandante Micky' Villa-lobos, the organiser of the invasion of the Agencias Graham, and his colleague 'Comandante Raul'. Yet, rather surprisingly, the housewives of the local mothers' committee (*central de madres*) expressed only contempt for the extremists. 'They are chickens,' they agreed, talking freely in the back room of a neighbourhood shop whose owner had frequently been threatened by local Socialists. 'They are brave when they come in a group of thirty, but in twos or threes they are nothing.'

The housewives did not like the new *canasta popular,* a form of rationing by which the supply committee (JAPs) organise the sale of a package of basic necessities through an official store at fixed prices. They complained that they had to buy the same things at the same time every week, regardless of whether they wanted (for example) a packet of soap powder that week, and of whether they actually had the money to pay for the goods on the day they were made available. They also complained that the system had been used by the Communists and Socialists to impose political controls. To qualify for the *canasta* in Lo Hermida, for instance, people were required to produce their electoral registration cards as well as their identity cards. The local JAPs had even begun to issue their own rationing cards, with the inscription, 'these cards come from the bases'.

The process of collecting the *canasta* was also fantastically time-consuming: the women spoke of having to queue from 6 in the morning until 6 at night in order to buy a single chicken. Worst of all, the local JAPs had begun to impose yet another condition: they were demanding that all adults who wished to qualify for the *canasta popular* should stand guard duty over the official store for several hours every week. This applied to women as well as men. The idea of serving guard duty in a vigilante group under Marxist control was so repugnant to many residents that some refused to do it although this meant that they had to resort to the black market and pay extortionate prices for some of their household necessities. It appeared that there had not been much physical intimidation in Lo Hermida, although two cases were cited to me of men who had had their arms broken for criticising the local JAPs. Despite the considerable risks of retaliation, many of the women from the *central de madres* that I talked with had put Frei posters up on their walls.

But how long could this show of political independence last after an election that had solved nothing? What I saw in Lo Hermida was merely a microcosm of what was taking place in all the working-class areas of Santiago: the creeping process of political control through the stomach, and the growing influence of the Marxist-dominated JAPs. The revolutionary tourists who came and went in Santiago, making much of the visible contrast between the cosmopolitan, affluent atmosphere of a middle-class *faubourg*-like Providencia and a working-class 'slum' like Lo Hermida failed to notice what was happening inside the *poblaciones* to muzzle those who dared to speak out against the 'workers' government'.

Two things happened shortly after the 4 March elections that provided some clues to the course that Chile might take. The first was the break-up of the MAPU, one of the smaller parties within Popular Unity that had, despite its diminutive size, contributed a great deal to government planning and had faithfully mirrored the divisions within the Marxist camp.

The rift took place almost immediately after the elections, and brought a *mafiosi* flavour to the internal politics of the Popular Unity coalition. Organised by Jaime Gazmuri and backed by Fernando Flores, MAPU's finance minister, about half of the party's central committee met on 7 March and declared the expulsion of twenty-five members, including Eduardo Aquevedo, a junior minister, and Oscar Garretón, the party's secretary-general. The victims of this committee decision had not been invited to attend the crucial meeting, and later charged that a quorum had not been present. Immediately after the vote, some of those present at the meeting drove off and occupied MAPU's central office in the Calle Principe de Gales, while others commandeered the official party cars and its radio station, Radio Candelaria. MAPU militants of the other faction tried, unsuccessfully, to prevent them from winning control of the party property, and Santiago by-passers were treated to the spectacle of two groups from a party within the ruling coalition fighting with each other in the streets.

For their part, the so-called *garretonistas* within the party proceeded to hold their own committee meeting in which they solemnly expelled Jaime Gazmuri and his colleagues, and proceeded to set up a new headquarters in the Calle Santa Lucia. Suddenly there were two MAPU parties where formerly there had been one, each headed by a young professional (Gazmuri was twenty-eight and a trained agricultural engineer; Garretón was twenty-nine and an economist in the same line as Vuskovic). The Communists and the Radicals were ready to accept Gazmuri; the Socialists and *Izquierda Cristiana* were inclined to side with Garretón. By the end of the month, it was still unclear which MAPU party was the official one, although all the MAPU members with prominent posts in the government (apart from Aquevedo) had tended to side with Gazmuri.

Now this case of 'popular disunity' amounted to more than political comic opera. The rift within the MAPU was an accurate reflection of the fault-line than ran through Allende's coalition as a whole and threatened to widen into an unbridgeable chasm. Gazmuri's wing of the party believed in the Communist thesis that it was necessary to pause and consolidate and at all costs to preserve the unity of the ruling coalition. Its members were ready to work with the armed forces; at any rate, like the Communists, they were determined not to give them any cause for anger. They were ready at least to consider the possibility of arriving at a new understanding with the Americans through the payment of some form of compensation for expropriated copper interests. Garretón's faction, in contrast, subscribed to the views of Altamirano and the Socialist left, and was militantly opposed to any form of compromise with the middle-class parties, the armed forces, or the Americans. It had close relations with the MIR, and like the *miristas*, had bitterly attacked the proposals of the Communist minister of economy, Orlando Millas, for the devolution of some industries taken over during or after the October strikes.

Garretón's views were reflected in the celebrated internal report of the MAPU party that had been leaked to *El Mercurio* shortly before the 4 March election. It was more than likely that it had in fact been the publication of this document that had triggered off the gang-war between the two factions in MAPU. Allende had been greatly angered by some of its contents—notably its implied criticism of the role of the military in the government and its admission of the government's culpability for the economic crisis—and to have urged the moderates within MAPU to take reprisals against those within the party who had been extreme enough to formulate these views and foolish enough to allow them to become public. Gazmuri's rigged committee meeting may have been held at Allende's personal instigation.

Whatever the truth of the matter, the MAPU split raised the bigger question of how long Popular Unity, which looked increasingly like a coalition of incompatibles, could be held together. Carlos Altamirano is said to have approached the three military ministers soon after the election results were announced and to have told them that there was now no reason why they should stay on in the government. In the immediate aftermath of the election, it was the relationship with the armed forces that polarised opinion within Allende's alliance. It may have been partly the desire to maintain the unity of the left that induced Allende to permit the military ministers to leave the cabinet on 22 March.

The formation of a new cabinet brought the first experiment in 'civil–military government' in Chile to an end. Many senior officers welcomed the resignation of the military ministers. They had grown progressively more disenchanted with Allende as it became plain that he was not ready to take firm action to curb the revolutionary left or to reconstruct the economy. They also felt that, now that the elections had been held peacefully, the main reason for the presence of the military in the government had disappeared. The resignation of the military ministers had become inevitable after Allende had refused—at the instigation of the Socialists—to accept a detailed list of demands that they had presented to him about a week after the elections. The key demands in this 'remonstrance' were: a law defining the public and private sectors of the economy; dialogue with opposition parties; suppression of armed para-military groups; and a new understanding with the United States. But it is significant that Allende made private assurances to the military leaders that he would find it easier to comply with at least some of their demands if they left the cabinet.

If the logic of that argument was not entirely clear at the time, it soon transpired that Allende interpreted his promises in a different way from the military. After he had formed a new cabinet (in which the replacements for the military ministers were relative nonentities best known for their loyalty to the president) he rushed through a new 'decree of insistence' in order to confiscate a further forty-one private firms and tabled a new education law, based on the ideas of an East-German adviser, that would have placed the school system under the control of Marxist ideologies. It aroused violent reactions from both the army and the church. Allende had decided not to call a halt to the revolution. And so much had already been changed in Chile that it could be said that he had partly succeeded in his aim of making his programme 'irreversible'.

N

CHAPTER NINE

Death in Santiago

The final phase of the Marxist experiment turned into a deadly competition between those who became convinced that violence was the only way to stop Chile's downhill slide towards civil war and those who were already convinced that violence was the only way to save the revolution from its enemies. The Marxist ultras now worked frenetically to complete their preparations for a left-wing coup (on the model of the Bolshevik revolution) that would pre-empt any eventual attempt at military intervention.

The full extent of these preparations was not accurately known until after the September coup, when the military junta claimed that it had discovered—in a safe in the office of the Communist under-secretary for the interior, Daniel Vergara—detailed plans for the assassination of hundreds of opposition leaders, senior officers, and conservative journalists and businessmen. This 'night of the long knives' was supposed to have taken place on Chile's independence day, less than a week after the coup.

The first news of this discovery was greeted with widespread scepticism, but the junta's claims gained in plausibility because the extreme left had already hatched similar, though smaller-scale, assassination plots. The junta also claimed that it had discovered, in the presidential palace alone, enough weapons to arm 1,000 men. It was not possible to confirm these reports at the time this chapter was written. But if they can be confirmed, they would mean that, if the armed forces had not moved on 11 September, the left would have staged a bloody pre-emptive strike that would have broken the back-bone of the opposition.

The period between the end of March and the September coup was a time of rising street violence, economic collapse and falling cabinets, in which Allende groped for a way to govern the country while the wild men on his left urged him to finish the revolution before the opposition geared itself up to finish with him. Late in April, he went down to the Communist-run labour ministry to parley with young militants of the Workers' Revolutionary Front (affiliated to the MIR) who had taken it over. They demanded to know why he had so far failed to shut down Congress. The pressure on Allende to move further and faster to complete the revolution now came from supposed 'moderates' within his coalition as well as from the ultras. In a rare display of unanimity, for example, the political commissions of both the Communist and Socialist Parties sent a joint memorandum to the president at the end of June that put an end to his early attempts to reach a negotiated settlement with the strikers at the El Teniente copper mine.

This was a time of rumour and panic reactions, in which every day brought new stories of intrigues among the officer corps or left-wing plots to assassinate opposition leaders or move armed brigades into downtown Santiago. Not for the first time, Allende tried to exploit the Reichstag fire technique in order to find scapegoats for the country's problems. Early in May, dark rumours of a right-wing plot to use Bolivian mercenaries and Brazilian money to topple the regime were given banner headlines in the pro-government press, and notably in *Ultima Hora,* a paper partly owned by Allende's fellow-Socialist and intimate friend, José Tohá. After the arrest of some forty members of the extreme right-wing movement *Patria y Libertad* on charges of conspiracy and the illegal possession of arms in the same month, Allende launched a campaign to proscribe it.

The strang behaviour of the deputy leader of *Patria y Libertad*, Roberto Thieme, lent some credence to govern-

ment claims that his movement was planning for some kind
of insurrection. He vanished on 23 February in a light plane
which was reported to have exploded and crashed into the
Pacific. It was suggested by other leaders of *Patria y Libertad*
at the time that Thieme had flown out to keep track of a
shipment of arms being smuggled into a clandestine Communist guerrilla group operating in the north of Chile by a
Russian submarine. It was even rumoured that his death
had been arranged by a KGB agent.

All this sounded like something out of Ian Fleming, but
Thieme's real story was hardly less colourful. After a public
funeral had been held for him, he turned up again in May
when his plane made an emergency landing near Mendoza
in Argentina. He was temporarily interned by the Argentine
authorities only to turn up in Chile later to organise the
sabotage of communications and vital services in support of
the truck-drivers' strike. Thieme's exact place in the tangled
undergrowth of Chilean politics in the months before the
coup remains mysterious. His melodramatic escapades helped
the government in its attempts to invoke the bogey of a
right-wing plot. He helped Allende even more by singing
like a bird after he was arrested in a fashionable German
restaurant in El Arrayán at the end of August. His willingness to talk, as well as the way he wantonly exposed himself
to the police, led some people to suggest that he was actually
a left-wing infiltrator.

But the escapades of the extreme right were trivial by
comparison with the sinister build-up of the armed workers'
brigades, and the changing mood within the officer corps.
The services, traditionally insulated from each other, had
been drawn closer together during the first civil–military
cabinet. Their awareness of the social and economic problems facing the country had been heightened by the reports
prepared by a group of independent and opposition economists who had been meeting on a weekly basis since January.
This group was to supply the key planners and economic
managers after Allende's fall. Early in June, a new attempt

was made to co-ordinate military thinking by setting up two special committees representing the three armed services— one at the level of generals, the other at the level of colonels. These developments cannot be interpreted as preparations for the coup, but they did help to establish a tactical unity among the senior commanders.

It was quite obvious even at the time when General Prats was minister of the interior that he was losing the confidence of his colleagues in the council of generals. The doubts of these officers were confirmed when the Supreme Court criticised him for having instructed the provincial *intendentes,* while he was interior minister, not to use the police to enforce court orders relating to the illegal seizure of farms. The first head-on collision between Prats and the council of generals came in June, when Allende—faced with a censure motion against his entire cabinet from Congress—was trying to coax the military back into the government to intimidate the opposition. On 27 June, the council of generals met to vote on Prats's suggestions for a new joint cabinet. Eighteen generals voted against; only six were in favour.

That same day, something happened in Santiago that did far more than any conflict of principles to discredit General Prats in the eyes of other officers. As he was driving in his official car past the expropriated breweries, Cervecerías Unidas, a middle-class woman, Sra Alejandrina Cox, spotted him from her passing car and stuck her tongue out at him. Prats ordered his driver to give pursuit, chased her for ten blocks in his car, fired two shots at her vehicle and finally, when she had been forced to stop, put his revolver to her forehead and addressed her as follows: 'Apologise you shit or I'll kill you.' ('*Pide perdon mierda o te mato.*') At least, that is how the unfortunate Sra Cox reported it, and her account was borne out by a letter Prats sent to her the following day. A hostile crowd gathered at once hurling abuse at the general—which the government later cited as evidence of a Schneider-style 'assassination plot' against Prats.

This was merely a way of saving face for the general. He had behaved in an amazing way for a commander-in-chief and despite the violent events of the following days, his fellow-officers never forgot or forgave it. Prats went to Allende in a highly emotional state and offered to resign. Allende refused his resignation, and for good reasons. He knew that the anti-Marxist generals would be reluctant to move against him so long as they thought that that would produce a split in the armed forces. So long as Prats remained in command, such a split would be unavoidable, since he had made it plain that he would not support an attempt to topple Allende. With Prats gone, however, the way would be open for united military action.

Two days after General Prats's encounter with Sra Cox, nonetheless, the government did have a *putsch* on its hands. Or so it seemed. But it is impossible to believe that Colonel Roberto Souper and the 420 men of his Second Tank Regiment (or rather, the 412 who actually participated) can really have been part of a serious plot to overthrow the regime. They were pawns in a game that they could not comprehend, and the hand manipulating them may well have been that of the Allende government itself, anxious to find a pretext for clamping down on the opposition elements in the armed forces.

Of Colonel Souper's motives there are no doubts: he was linked by personal conviction and family ties to *Patria y Libertad*. But his decision to drive into the centre of Santiago and station his tanks in front of the presidential palace and the defence ministry was taken without consulting other units. It is not clear just what he thought he might achieve. The only thing he succeeded in doing was to release—temporarily at least—a young officer of his regiment, Captain Rocha, who was being held under arrest in the defence ministry.

What does seem clear is that the government had prior warning of Souper's intentions. The Second Tank Regiment moved on La Moneda at 9 o'clock on the morning of 29

June, picking its way through the morning rush-hour traffic.
At 8.15 am, José Tohá, the defence minister and General
Pickering, a leading pro-Allende general, had already set up
an emergency headquarters in the defence academy. This
may indicate that Colonel Souper was deluded into thinking
that a coup was in motion, although the evidence is not yet
complete. At any rate, his pitiful gesture, which ended after
barely two hours of desultory fighting when he meekly handed
over his sword to General Prats, enabled the commander-in-
chief to recover some of the prestige he had lost earlier in the
week.

The left-wing press duly hailed General Prats as the
'saviour' of Santiago. There was a sombre footnote to the
farce, however, in the savage repression of those members of
the Second Tank Regiment who had remained at their
barracks, and this was held against Prats by some of his
fellow-officers.[1] The most sinister side-effect of the day's
charade was that the extreme left gave a glimpse of its
arsenal: Souper's men were fired upon by armed government supporters from the windows of ministries and state-
run firms near La Moneda, and armed workers responded to
an appeal to mobilise in the factories. Some 300 small private
firms were grabbed on the day of Souper's 'coup'.

History, according to Marx, begins as tragedy and ends as
farce. In Chile, it happened the other way round. Chile was
no banana republic where an erratic colonel could topple a
regime while the peasants kept on tilling their fields. Allende
could only be overthrown by a disciplined action of the
armed forces as a whole, backed up by a powerful section of
Chilean society. To understand how those conditions came
about, it is necessary to look first at the failure of Allende's
second experiment with a Marxist–military alliance, and
then at the events that finally persuaded the high command
to act.

On 5 July, Allende managed to cobble together a new
civilian cabinet in which each of the Popular Unity parties
was given its customary weighting. The interesting feature

of this cabinet was that the vital interior ministry went to Carlos Briones, a criminologist associated with the Socialist Party who was respected by many opposition leaders as a man with a degree of respect for due legal process that was a rare quality among his Marxist colleagues. The Briones appointment was one sign of a new attempt to woo the centre.

But Allende had failed in his efforts to get Christian Democrats into the new cabinet. He had again been making advances to left-wing advocates of 'dialogue' in Frei's party— to Radomiro Tomic, Bernardo Leighton and Renan Fuentealba. But the Christian Democratic party was by now fairly solidly behind its strong-willed new president, Patricio Aylwin, a strong Frei supporter who would not tolerate a backroom deal with Allende. A *freista* who had been a junior minister in the previous government summed up the party's mood as follows: 'My impression is that the real bases of the party want to negotiate with the military to form a government without Allende and without the right.'

Having failed to co-opt the left of the Christian Democratic Party, Allende turned back to the armed forces when a major strike movement got underway at the end of the month. The pattern of events was oddly reminiscent of what happened in October. The truck-drivers' union got the ball rolling with a new strike that started on 25 July as a protest against persisting shortages of spare parts, official discrimination in favour of state-run firms and the effects of inflation on frozen tariffs. Other groups, like the shopkeepers, taxi-drivers and professional *colegios,* joined in; the government blamed the wave of violent incidents that accompanied the strikes on 'fascist conspirators'; and in the end the armed forces were brought back into the cabinet to restore confidence, to the confusion of both the right and the extreme left.

It was a considerable triumph both for Allende and Prats that the military were induced to return to the cabinet on 9 August, despite the fact that some days earlier the Christian Democrats had urged the government to appoint generals to key ministries in order to restore calm in the midst of a series of bombings and street-battles. The murder of Allende's naval aide-de-camp, Captain Araya, at the end of July had convinced many officers that the government was unwilling to clamp down on left-wing terrorists. Although the government tried to blame the murder on the extreme right (and Carlos Altamirano even accused *El Mercurio* of being its 'intellectual author') the only people actually charged with the crime turned out to be left-wing extremists, including a certain José Luis Riquelme, affiliated with the MIR. The president of the special military commission of inquiry set up by Allende, Air-Force General Nicanor Diaz Estrada, bitterly attacked the left-wing chief of *Investigaciones* when he claimed on television early in August that the crime had been almost solved.[2]

In the August reshuffle, all four service chiefs (counting the head of the paramilitary Carabineros) were appointed to the cabinet. General Prats took over the ministry of defence; General José Mario Sepulveda, chief of the Carabineros, took over the ministry of lands and colonisation; Air-Force General César Ruiz Danyau became minister of transport and public works; and Admiral Raúl Montero took over the finance ministry. The news of these appointments did not bring rejoicing to the opposition, which was baffled by the intentions of the high command, and it did not bring a halt to the strikes, now said to be costing the country $5 million a day. Ex-president Frei pointed out that the armed forces had not clearly established the basis for their participation in the new cabinet and that Admiral Montero, as a man without specialist economic training, would find it very hard to deal with the Communists in control of the Central Bank and the key economic agencies.

It appears that the military themselves were uncertain of their new role. Of the four military ministers, two (Prats and Sepulveda) were strong Allende supporters, one (Ruiz) was highly critical of the government and the last (Montero) was in a shaky middle position and distrusted by many of his senior subordinates. The new cabinet fell apart in less than a fortnight, when Allende prised General Ruiz out of his air-force job. Ruiz had an impossible task in negotiating with the striking truck-drivers through his under-secretary, Jaime Faivovich, a Socialist extremist who believed that the solution was to use troops to confiscate their lorries. General Ruiz handed in his resignation as minister after only nine days, on the ground that he had been 'unable to achieve his objectives'.

Ruiz found, however, that Dr Allende was waiting to accept his resignation as commander of the air force. He hinted on television the following night that he had been arbitrarily sacked, and his air-force colleagues rallied to his support. On Monday, 20 August, while the president was down south in Chillán, an air-force colonel called Ramon Gallegos announced that the service intended to protest against the injury done to its 'sole and authentic commander'. The air-force commanders were shrewd enough not to follow this up without the support of the other services, but by the time that General Gustavo Leigh formally took over Ruiz's job that Monday night, the political atmosphere in Santiago was frenzied. The left-wing leaders of the CUT called, as they had done during previous crises, for the workers to stand guard in their factories.

But the long-term significance of the Ruiz sacking was that it further undermined the confidence of the army and the navy in their commanding officers. The air force had stood solidly behind Ruiz; General Leigh, a tough, athletic former military attaché in Washington, shared Ruiz's view of the situation and was very reluctant to take over his job.[3] But General Prats and Admiral Montero had done nothing more than make a token offer to resign when their colleague was sacked. Allende did throw them a sop: General Brady was appointed to replace Faivovich as the government negotiator with the strikers. But in the eyes of many officers, Prats and Montero had failed in their duty to defend their fellow-commander against a political 'purge'.

Events now moved quickly to a climax. The strike move-

ment continued to broaden; armed clashes of rival bands of
demonstrators in the Santiago streets were followed by the
fire-bombing of the local branch of the CUT, controlled by
Christian Democrats; and on 22 August, Congress passed a
crucial resolution. The Chamber of Deputies ruled that the
government had gravely violated the constitution, and
addressed a direct appeal to the military ministers. 'It is a
fact,' the resolution ran, 'that the present government, from
the beginning, has attempted to seize total power, with the
evident purpose of subjecting everyone to the most rigorous
economic and political controls, and of achieving by this
means the installation of a totalitarian absolutely opposed
to the system of representative democracy that the constitution upholds.' The Chamber ruled that

> the armed forces and the Carabineros must be a guarantee
> to all Chileans and not just to a section of the country or
> a political combination. Therefore, they should not parti-
> cipate in the government in order to support the policy
> of a sectarian minority, but in order to re-establish the
> rule of the constitution and the law . . . in order to guaran-
> tee institutional stability, civil peace, security and develop-
> ment.[4]

This resolution, which catalogued the government's
illegal acts, was carried by 81 votes to 47. It was later debated
whether in any sense it provided a *legal* basis for military
intervention. It did not have the force of law. Under the
Chilean constitution, a two-thirds majority is required to
impeach the president although it is worth remembering (as
opposition jurists were pointing out before the coup) that
under Article 43 the president can be declared 'unfit for
office'—on mental or physical grounds—by a simple majority
and thus compelled to step down. The important thing about
the 22 August resolution was that it could be interpreted as
a *moral* basis for military intervention, so long as it was
intended to 're-establish the rule of the constitution and the

law'. Thus it marked a major turning-point in the relationship between Congress and the armed forces.

The following day, 23 August, the council of generals
forced General Prats to resign as commander-in-chief. The
day before, some 300 officers' wives (including the wives of
senior generals) had demonstrated noisily outside his home
in Las Condes, demanding that he should go. Not for the
first time in Allende's Chile, the women played a decisive
role in changing things. Someone remarked that the only
Chilean party worth belonging to was the party of the
women. The author was reminded of a pro-Allende rally in
April when columns of tough workers from the *cordones,*
including some Cubans and some Dominican exiles, marched
through Providencia shouting *'Si los momios quieren guerra,
guerra los tendrán.'* ('If the reactionaries want war, they shall
have it.') A single girl walked out into the street in front of
them and shouted back, waving her fist, *'Y los momios lo
ganarán.'* ('And the reactionaries will win.') Nothing could
have showed up more dramatically than the wives' demonstration how deeply discredited General Prats had become
in the eyes of his officers. Allende was forced to bow to military pressure and accept his resignation. Two other pro-
Allende generals, Guillermo Pickering and Mario Sepulveda
(commander of the Santiago garrison) chose to resign with
him.

If one single event cleared the way for the September
coup, this was it. The armed forces were no longer subject
to a man who had been loyal to Allende in all things, out of
a mixture of opportunism, political ambition, and shared
ideals. Prats's successor, General Augusto Pinochet Ugarte,
did not share the same commitment to the regime.

The second Marxist–military cabinet fell apart completely
on 27 August, when Admiral Montero resigned as finance
minister. To the amazement of most observers, a new cabinet
was set up the following day. It again included four military
ministers, although only General Sepulveda of the Carabineros
was a service chief. But Allende had not pulled off a hat-trick.

The new cabinet was merely a decoy. By the time its members were announced, the minds of the men who organised the coup were already made up. When the tanks started to roll out into the streets at 4am on 11 September, everything had been carefully prepared. The air force had even stocked up with the bombs (purchased in Spain) that were dropped on La Moneda. Most important of all, when the orders went out, the high command did not split. Admiral Montero had already been given his marching orders by his senior officers on 31 August, although Allende, fearful of the man in line to replace him, refused to accept his resignation. On the day of the coup, Montero was content to step aside to make way for Admiral Torribio Merino Castro, the commander of the squadron in Valparaiso, whose driving force was one of the main influences behind the coup. Similarly, General Sepulveda was brushed aside by a more combative and anti-Marxist Carabinero general, César Mendoza Durán.

The high command decided to overthrow Allende for a combination of reasons. The generals had despaired long ago of the government's ability to handle the crippling economic crisis and to negotiate a solution for the strikes that had held up vital copper shipments and raised the spectre of famine when grain supplies were held up in the docks. They had become deeply suspicious of the Marxists' ultimate aims. More important still, they had come under tremendous civilian pressure to act. The degree of popular backing for the coup was demonstrated afterwards when it was applauded by the leaders of both the National and Christian Democratic Parties and by the *gremialistas*. Even Cardinal Silva Enriquez, who had played a somewhat ambiguous role as a mediator between the Allende government and the Christian Democrats, gave qualified approval for the coup, while the Communist union leader, Jorge Godoy, urged the workers to remain calm.

But the immediate trigger for the coup stemmed from a series of head-on collisions between individual officers and the extreme left. Some of these resulted from the increasing determination with which the armed forces policed the law that gave them responsibility for arms control. Early in August, a worker called Manuel Gonzales Bustamente was shot dead by troops searching for concealed weapons in a textile factory in the southern town of Punta Arenas. Socialist politicians chose this as the pretext to hurl abuse at the conservative commander of the Fifth Division, stationed in the area. General Manuel Torres de la Cruz was denounced by the large and voluble Socialist deputy Mario Palestro (who looked and often sounded like Pancho Villa) as a 'satrap, a megalomaniac and a madman'. The armed forces brought charges against Palestro for defaming their institutions.

Far more serious than this exchange of insults was the discovery by naval intelligence of a plot to promote a rebellion among sailors on board the cruiser 'Latorre', stationed off Valparaiso, and units based at Talcahuano farther south. The plot involved the murder of officers in their beds, and the bombardment of shore installations by the ships that the rebels hoped to capture. Some 300 sailors (mostly ordinary ratings under the age of twenty-five) were arrested and interrogated. Left-wing leaders claimed that some of the prisoners were subsequently tortured and that, far from being involved in a mutiny, they had tried to disrupt preparations for a coup. The navy appealed to the Supreme Court and Congress to suspend the parliamentary immunity of Carlos Altamirano and the MAPU leader, Oscar Garretón, who were charged (along with Miguel Enriquez of the MIR) with being the 'intellectual authors' of the plot. This, in turn, provoked violent left-wing demonstrations in Valparaiso that pitted *miristas* manning freshly-built barricades against the naval garrison.

The troubles in Valparaiso came on top of rumours that the government was nursing plans for a purge—and possibly the purge by assassination—of known anti-Allende officers in the armed forces. One story frequently heard in the messes was that during the visit of the Cuban leader, Carlos Rafael Rodriguez, in June, the government had drawn up a list of seven army generals, four admirals and two air-force generals who should be removed as 'a matter of utmost urgency'. Whether or not there was substance to these stories, it was clear that the armed forces could not stand by indefinitely if their careers, military discipline, and perhaps their lives as well, were endangered. The navy, with first-hand experience of a left-wing attempt to destroy the armed forces from within, now took the lead in pressing for the coup. It was not by accident that the signal for the coup was given by a rising of the naval garrison at Valparaiso on Monday, 10 September.

The collapse of Chile's Marxist experiment was foreshadowed by a chilling phrase that had cropped up amongst the dense foliage of political slogans on the Santiago walls early in 1972. The words *'Ya viene Djakarta'* ('Djakarta is coming') were exotic and probably incomprehensible to most Chileans. But the purge of the Indonesian Communists after the failure of their plot to assassinate the generals who had been more or less content, up to that moment in 1965, to play along with Sukarno, bore a striking resemblance to what later took place in Chile—although the cost, in terms of human lives, was infinitely less the second time round.

The military government established by General Pinochet and his colleagues promised to 'eradicate Marxism'. But it had to confront, with limited forces,[5] determined resistance from armed workers in the state-run industries, from a sophisticated Communist cell network in Santiago, and from long-established guerrilla groups in the south. It remained to be seen whether left-wing predictions that Chile would become a 'second Vietnam' would prove to be accurate. The new government faced enormous problems, quite apart from the armed resistance of the left: the need to find a formula for stable government in a highly politicised country, to restructure the civil administration, to rebuild the economy and to improve its image in the outside world. Its ultimate success was bound to depend to a large degree on whether it could keep the support of its civilian backers and enlist foreign aid in quantities that Allende was never quite able to extract from his Soviet patrons.

Paradoxically, Salvador Allende, who began by bitterly attacking the economic dependency of Chile on western sources of capital and technology, ended by courting the Russians in pursuit of an even greater degree of economic dependency on the Communist bloc. It was said that, during his visit to Moscow in December 1972, he had hoped to receive credits and hard-currency loans from the Russians totalling $500 million. Over the period before Allende's visit, he had received some $400 million from Russia, but much of this total took the form of project aid and tied import credits.

The Russians clearly had an important stake in Chile. It was after all a test-tube demonstration of a Marxist government controlling a democratic society, and the success or failure of Allende's experiment would be certain to stir ripples in France and Italy—amongst the socialist intelligentsia, if not among ordinary voters. And there was also the consoling thought that Chile was basically a much richer country than Cuba, with a major export commodity (copper) that could find a much wider market than Cuban sugar. Maybe Chile would not turn into a pensioner on the Cuban model—at least not after an initial period of adjustment. Finally, the Russians must have become increasingly convinced, as reports flowed in of the success of the Chilean Marxists in destroying the private sector of the economy, that the classic formula for the conquest of political power through the seizure of economic power was actually beginning to work out, and that Chile might eventually be transformed into a faithful, if distant, satellite. True, Chile could hardly be counted crucial to the balance of power—not even to the regional balance of power—but it might provide a very useful launching-pad for Communist subversion in neighbouring countries. Under the Allende government, as has been noted, the Cubans used Santiago as a base for training and indoctrinating exile groups from a number of other

Latin-American countries, especially groups from Bolivia.

All these were reasons why the Russians might have been expected to bail Allende out. And yet he returned from Moscow a visibly disappointed man at the end of 1972. He had obtained a limited amount of aid in the form of tied credits and also some $50 million in military credits—which may have appeared less than useful to him, since he knew that if he attempted to make use of these, he might come under attack by senior officers (especially in the navy and air force) for attempting to tie Chile's weapons systems to those of the Soviet Union. The full details of Allende's agreement in Russia were not publicly divulged. It is probable that he also received enough cash (in the form of hard-currency loans) to tide him over the pre-election period. But the country's foreign reserves were exhausted by the beginning of April. Allende did not return to Santiago empty-handed, but he did not return with the largesse he had hoped for.

There are three possible explanations for the Russians' apparent stinginess, and probably all three at least partially apply. First, it may have been that—despite all other considerations—the Russians were by no means anxious to over-commit themselves afresh by pumping aid into a dubious beneficiary. Their generous aid to Egypt had not, for example, bought them the unconditional loyalty that they may have hoped for. Second, the Russians may have had their own conditions to put to Allende—notably, that his government should set about rebuilding the domestic economy according to orthodox guidelines—and may not have been entirely satisfied with his response. Third, it was even more likely that the Russians had arrived at some kind of understanding with the Americans over Chile. At a time when the Russians were not doing at all badly in the course of east–west negotiations on trade and security and had just received the promise of an enormous American wheat shipment to help them over a bad harvest, they were probably not anxious to annoy President Nixon by interfering too blatantly in Chile.

P

Whatever their real motives, the position that the Russians adopted made it uncertain whether Allende would be able to find the outside sources of finance that would enable him to cover the mounting budgetary deficit and pay for imports in 1973, while it was equally uncertain whether he would be able to count on as much tolerance from Chile's creditors when it came to renegotiating the country's external debt as he had been able to draw upon in 1972. Looking at the state of the economy after the fall of the Marxist government, it was clear to any unblinkered observer that whatever government was to rule Chile in the ensuing years, it would need to be able to enlist massive outside help to rebuild what had been broken down.

This book should not end with predictions about the future after Allende. But the previous chapters have provided some basis for judging the Marxist experiment. Many outsiders persist in seeing Allende as a progressive reformer, the victim of 'monopolistic conspiracies', 'American imperialism', or the intrigues of an ultra-reactionary clique. The word 'reformer' does not apply to Allende. One distinguished Latin-American political scientist who thought that it did (writing early in 1972) suggested that political reform could be defined by four basic characteristics: (i) the 'maintenance or consolidation of political democracy'; (ii) the 'promotion or acceleration of economic development'; (iii) the nationalist re-orientation of the economy and of 'the whole society in general'; and (iv) the enlargement of the 'socio-economic participation' of the rural masses (through agrarian reform) and of the urban masses (through more employment opportunities and higher welfare payments).[6]

How many of these characteristics applied to Allende's Chile? Far from 'maintaining and consolidating' the country's democratic system, Allende's government rode roughshod over it and the Marxist ultras proceeded to create, in the form of neighbourhood committees like the JAPs and militant workers' organisations like the comandos comunales, parallel institutions intended to usurp the functions of the administration. The course that they steered led inevitably to a violent confrontation. Far from promoting economic development, the government's policies created the worst economic crisis in Chile since the Great Depression. The Allende government could, it is true, lay claim to having carried out a 'nationalist re-orientation' of the country through the attack on western investors and radical foreign policy gestures such as the recognition of Cuba. But the state of the economy, it has been suggested, was leading the country towards an even greater measure of dependence on the Soviet bloc— if only the Russians would produce the goods! Finally, Allende could certainly pride himself on having enlarged the 'socio-economic participation' of lower-income groups, but the methods employed involved a tremendous social and economic cost. That cost, it has been argued in this book, was held by the Marxist strategists to be worth paying not as the cost of meaningful reform but as the cost of transforming Chile from a pluralistic democracy into a monolithic state ruled by a narrow ideological elite.

Theirs was a programme for power, not philanthropy. Their rapid gains over the three years of Allende's rule did not augur well for other societies that might be led to adopt the 'Chilean way'. The chief reason why Chile matters to the outside world is not that events have changed the strategic balance in Latin America. It is that in Chile, a Marxist strategy for the conquest of political power from within a democratic system came dangerously close to success. The lesson, and the warning, can hardly be neglected by those countries that could one day find themselves confronted with a similar set of circumstances. It is profoundly to be hoped that Chile's tragedy, resulting in the temporary death of democracy, will not be repeated. But it must not be forgotten who was primarily responsible for it.

Notes to this chapter are on page 215

Notes

CHAPTER ONE

1 Tuchnin, R., in *Izvestia*, 13 December 1970
2 Quoted in Luis Corvalán, *Camino de Victoria* (Santiago 1971) p23
3 Quoted by Academician N. Inozemtzev in his article, 'The Principledness and Effectiveness of Soviet Foreign Policy' in *Pravda*, 9 June 1972. For a useful discussion of Soviet reactions to Allende's victory, see Gouré, Leon and Suchliki, Jaime, 'The Allende Regime: Actions and Reactions' in *Problems of Communism*, May–June 1971 pp49–61
4 'Mensaje al Congreso del Presidente Salvador Allende'. Reprinted as supplement to *Punto Final*, 8 June 1971
5 Interview with Ismael Weinberger in *El Popular* (Montevideo) 5 November 1970
6 Labarca, Eduardo, *Corvalán 27 Horas* (Santiago 1972) pp110–12; 104–5
7 On 6 April 1972, for example, after the decision of the recently-formed Left Radical Party (PIR) to leave the government, Allende announced a plan to dissolve Congress. If Congress persisted in an 'obstructionist attitude towards the executive,' he declared, he would ask it to vote for its own dissolution. If this was rejected, he would call for a referendum. At this stage, such threats were no more than hot air, but they gave a pretty clear idea of Allende's own attitude towards the country's parliamentary institutions, *El Mercurio*, 7 April 1972
8 See Debray, Régis, *Conversations with Allende* (1971)
9 Quoted in MacHale, Tomás P., *El Frente de la libertad de expresión* (Santiago 1972)
10 See Orrego, Claudio, 'Los Fundamentos Ideológicos de la Estrategia UP' in *Chile: El Costo Social de la Dependencia Ideológica* (Santiago 1973) p20
11 Jobet, Julio César, 'El Partido socialista de Chile' (*Prensa Latina Americana*, Santiago 1971) p172

206

12 Corvalán has provided an interesting summary of the Communist view of 'orderly revolution': 'We are partisans of social discipline within the framework of the struggle for the fulfilment of the programme... We believe in avoiding, so far as possible, all strikes while there is a People's Government, since these affect production in one way or another... We will maintain our struggle against the ultra-left (*ultraizquierda*) as against any other manifestation of opportunism in the midst of the popular movement... This is the only correct line and I believe it will end in victory.' *Corvalán 27 Horas* op cit, pp122-3

13 For a somewhat different version of Chile's political evolution since November 1970, see the confidential analysis by the MAPU Party, 'Informe Confidencial del MAPU: La Unidad Popular al Desnudo' as published in *El Mercurio*, 1 March 1973. The authenticity of this document was admitted by the party's political commission (*El Mercurio*, 3 March 1973) and its publication may have contributed to the internal crisis that led to the break-up of MAPU shortly after the elections

14 *El Mercurio* (International edition) 25-30 September 1972

CHAPTER TWO

1 See Fontaine, Arturo, 'Revolución en Papel Sellado' in *Visión Crítica de Chile* (Santiago 1972) p66

2 Formed in 1966 from the fusion of the Conservative and Liberal Parties and the supporters of the independent right-wing politician Jorge Prat.

3 *La Nueva República: Programa del Partido Nacional de Chile* (Santiago 1970) p94

4 Electoral propaganda on both sides was fairly extreme. Posters appeared showing Soviet tanks in front of the La Moneda palace as part of a right-wing 'campaign of terror'.

5 Debray, Régis, *Conversations with Allende* (1972) p89

6 *Documentos Secretos de la ITT* (Santiago 1972)

7 Ibid, pp14, 40

8 Memo from W. R. Merriam to John McCone (ex-director of the CIA, dated 9 October 1970. *Documentos Secretos* p34

9 For a Cuban account of Cruz's activities, see *Bohemia* (Havana) 18 December 1970

10 The plan for the Schneider abduction seems to have closely followed the pattern of the so-called 'Colliguay plot' of 1951. That involved the kidnapping of two trade union leaders by right-wing extremists (apparently with their tacit consent). The kidnappers hoped that the left would blame the abduction on the government and call a general strike that could then be crushed. The hostages were found by the police before the other

union leaders had made up their minds how to respond. It is significant that Juan Diego Dávila was a key organiser in both conspiracies. See Hugh Bicheno's valuable article, 'Anti-parliamentary Themes in Chilean History' in Medhurst, K., (ed) *Allende's Chile* (1972)

11 *El Mercurio*, 7 May 1970

12 There is an interesting account by a prominent Communist journalist. See Eduardo Labarca Goddard, *Chile al Rojo* (Santiago 1971)

13 Partido Socialista de Chile, *Estatutos y programa* (Santiago 1936)

14 Quoted in Thomas, Hugh, *The Spanish Civil War* (Penguin edition, 1965) p130

15 See Laferrte, Elias, *Vida de un comunista* (Santiago 1961) for the 'official' Communist version. Marcos Chamudes, *Chile: Una Advertencia Americana* (Ediciones PEC, Santiago 1972) is enlightening on Ravines's 1935 trip and on other aspects of his mission. There is also Ravines's own self-apologia, *La Gran Estafa* (Santiago 1954)

16 Halperin, Ernst, *Nationalism and Communism in Chile* (Cambridge, Mass 1965) p42

17 The Socialists' 1939 'Plan for National Economic Action' had called, for example, for the distribution of land to the tiller, and the nationalisation of the banks. See Jobet, Julio César, 'El Partido Socialista y el Frente Popular en Chile' in *Arauco* No 85, February 1967, pp13–47

18 *El Siglo*, 23 June 1969

19 Jobet, Julio César, 'El Partido Socialista de Chile' (*Prensa Latino-Americana* (Santiago 1971) Vol 1, p130

20 'Declaración Político-Ideológica Aprobada en la XXV Convención Nacional del Partido Radical de Chile'. Reprinted in *Nueva Sociedad* (San José, Costa Rica) July–August 1972

21 *La Nación*, 8 August 1971

22 *Corvalán 27 Horas* op cit, p79

23 See, for example, Corvalán, Luis, 'Acerca de la Via Pacifica' in *Principios*, January 1961

24 See Manns, Patricio, *La Revolución de la Escuadra* (Universidad de Valparaiso 1972)

25 Chamudes, *Chile*, p81

26 *Nuestra Epoca* No 12, December 1962

27 Chamudes, Marcos, *El Libro Blanco de mi Leyenda Negra* (Santiago 1964) p10

28 Cantero was considered a possible successor to Corvalán. Among the other leading contenders, Millas was probably disqualified because of his unpopularity with the Socialists, and Volodia Teitelboim—probably the most versatile among the Communist leaders—was counted out both because he was regarded as an arch pro-Soviet and, ironically, because he was Jewish (which, as Jewish ex-Communists in Chile have testified, has been used against them by the most reactionary sections of the Party)

29 Neruda, Pablo, *Incitación al Nixonicidio y Alabanza de la Revolución*, Chilean poems (Quimantú, Santiago 1973)
30 *El Siglo*, 29 March 1962
31 Ibid
32 Carlos Altamirano, paradoxically, was one of those who supported collaboration with Ibáñez
33 Quoted in *Ercilla*, 'El Lado Oculto del P.S.' 13 September 1972
34 Jobet, *El Partido Socialista*, I, p130
35 *Punto Final*, 13 February 1973 (Supplement)

CHAPTER THREE

1 For a colourful, though not entirely reliable, guide to the personal backgrounds of the technocratic 'new class', see Valdés, Jaime, *La 'Clase' dorada (o el Giobierno secreto de la UP)* (Santiago 1973)
2 The survey was conducted in the UNICOOP stores
3 *El Mercurio*, 26 February 1972. It is worth comparing the record of central planning in Chile with Allende's assertion (in his message to Congress on 21 May 1971) that 'no investment decision should be taken unless it is included in the plans centrally approved by the government'.
4 *Comentarios Sobre la Situación Económica* (2nd semester 1972). Taller de Coyuntura, Departamento de Economía, Universidad de Chile (Santiago 1963) p5
5 Ibid p3. See also de Castro, Sergio, (ed) *Analisis de la Economía Chilena 1971–2* (Universidad Católica de Chile, April 1972) and *Informe de Coyuntura No 2* (Sociedad de Fomento Fabril, June 1972)
6 Quoted in Labrousse, Alain, *L'Expérience Chilienne* (Seuil, Paris 1972) p262
7 This document is printed as an appendix to Rodríguez, Pablo, *Entre la Democracia y la Tirania* (Santiago 1972)
8 *Kommunist*, No 3, 1972 (Moscow)
9 By October 1972, the state was estimated to control directly 90 per cent of the mining industry; 85 per cent of all banking; 60 per cent of large-scale commerce; 52 per cent of manufacturing industry; 84 per cent of the construction industry; and 75 per cent of agricultural land had been brought into the 'reformed area'.
10 See 'El Poder de Dirinco' in *Que Pasa*, 19 October 1972
11 *Diario Oficial*, 4 April 1972
12 Centro de Estudios de la Revolución, *CER* Año II, No 3
13 As long ago as 1958, it was calculated that a drop of 1 per cent per pound in the world price of Chilean copper would cost the country $7 million in foreign exchange earnings and a further $7 million in revenues from copper. (See Gil, Federico G., *The*

Political System of Chile (Boston 1966) p98. In the first quarter
of 1973, a rise of 1 per cent per pound would have been worth
a total of about $18 million.

14 *Copper is the Wage of Chile* (American Universities Field Staff
Reports Vol XIX No 3, 1972); Molina, Sergio, 'El Cobre: Per-
spectivas y Responsibilidades' in *Mensaje* (Santiago, September–
October 1971) and Carlos Correa Iglesias' two articles in *Portada*
Nos 33 and 34 (Santiago 1972)

15 Molina, op cit

16 The nationalisation of copper was later the theme of the decora-
tion on the new 500-escudo banknotes that Allende ordered to be
issued for the first time, as inflation soared.

17 *Latin America* (London) 23 March 1973

18 'Chuquicamata por Dentro', *El Mercurio*, 23–25 December 1971

19 One further example might be added to Carlos Correa's account.
Anaconda had invested in 35 enormous Lectron–Haul trucks
shortly before nationalisation, at a cost of some $263,000 each. A
single tyre for one of these trucks is almost three yards high and
costs $4,000. Yet, early in 1972, 18 of them—more than half—were
out of action due to 'maintenance and operational problems'.

20 'El Teniente por Dentro', *El Mercurio*, 13–15 February 1972

21 *La Prensa*, 22 February 1972

22 Emilio Sanfuentes, 'La política económica de la Unidad Popular',
in *Visión Crítica de Chile* (Santiago 1972)

23 *La Prensa*, 24 February 1972

24 *El Mercurio*, 16 April 1973

25 *La Prensa*, 23 February 1972

26 *Que Pasa*, 21 September 1972

CHAPTER FOUR

1 The best guides to the earlier experiments in agrarian reform are:
Kaufman, Robert R., *The Politics of Land Reform in Chile
1950–1970* (Cambridge, Mass 1972); Baraona, Pablo, 'Crisis de la
Agricultura Chilena' in *Visión Crítica,* op cit; Rogers, Jorge, *Dos
Caminos para la Reforma Agraria en Chile, 1945–1965* (Santiago
1966) and Varela, Luis Quiros, 'Chile: Agrarian Reform and Political Processes' in Medhurst, Kenneth, (ed) *Allende's Chile* (1972)

2 In 1941, for example, a Popular Front government issued an
executive order banning the formation of peasant unions. It was
not until 1947 that the government of President González Videla
issued a new law permitting peasant syndicates, subject to fairly
stringent qualifications. It was the Frei government that really
brought the peasants into politics by speeding up the process of
rural unionisation.

3 See Chonchol, Jacques, 'La Política Agrícola en una Economía de

Transición al Socialismo' in *Pensamiento Económico del Gobierno de Allende* (Santiago 1971)

4 Chonchol has cited a survey carried out in 1968 that showed that, out of 15,621 people working in a sample group of *asentamientos*, a third were landless labourers employed by members of the co-operative on very low wages. *La Nación*, 5 September 1971. See also Chonchol's interview with *Marcha* (Montevideo) 4 October 1971

5 A meeting organised by the militant 'Nuevo Horizonte' peasant federation (aligned with the MCR) at Arica in February 1972, proposed to reduce the size of estates in the arid northern provinces of Atacama and Tarapaca to 5 basic hectares. See *Punto Final*, 29 February 1972

6 For a useful discussion of these and similar cases, see 'Grupos Armados: Como Controlarlos' in *Qué Pasa*, 4 May 1972

7 Chonchol, 'Poder y Reforma Agraria en la Experiencia Chilena' in Anibal Pinto et al, *Chile Hoy* (Siglo Veintiuno, Santiago 1971) p318

8 See *El Siglo*, 14 August 1972 and *El Mercurio*, 16 August 1972. The Communist deputy and economist, Jose Cademartori, also attacked the inaccurate production estimates of the Agrarian Planning Office.

9 Sources: Central Bank for 1969–70; Instituto de Economía, Universidad Católica de Chile; Sociedad de Fomento Fabril and Taller de Coyuntura, Facultad de Ciencias Economicas, U. de Chile for 1971–2

10 Taller de Coyuntura, Dept de Economía, *Comentarios Sobre la Situación Económica*, 2nd semester 1972

11 Figures provided by the Colegio de Ingenieros Agrónomos. The Socialist daily, *Ultima Hora*, claimed that wheat imports in 1972 would cost around $60 million (26 September 1972). The National Society of Agriculture (SNA) claimed that the cost in 1973 would be twice as much.

12 See 'Producción Agricola Bajara 20% entre 1971 y 1973' in *Que Paso*, 1 February 1973

13 'Causas del Retroceso y de la Futura Crisis de la Agricultura Chilena'. Reprinted in *El Mercurio*, 11 March 1973. It is worth noting that a study by experts from the FAO, working with Chilean officials from the government agency ICIRA, that was presented to the minister of agriculture in November 1972 concluded that the land reform programme had resulted in the following things: (i) there was no increase in production; (ii) the system did not allow for satisfactory participation by the peasants; (iii) demand for food had risen; (iv) agricultural imports provided a third of internal food consumption in 1972; (v) despite falling production, these imports would have to be cut back because of the lack of foreign exchange; (vi) a general system of food rationing would have to be introduced; (vii) food production

Q

would have to rise by 50 per cent over the next four years to satisfy demand; (viii) The Agrarian Reform programme had as its sole aim the destruction of the big estates and lost sight of broader and more essential goals.

14 See the report in *Ercilla*, 21 March 1973

CHAPTER FIVE

1 See Chapter 7
2 He is quoted as having told them that the ideal drink quota for Chileans was two (small) bottles of beer a week, 'which is what the Cubans are given'. He warned that, if they drank too much, the workers would not be able to 'make babies', and based his advice 'not on my personal experience, but on my training as a doctor'.
3 Similar militias were formed late in 1972 in other construction companies, for instance, in COHABIT and CORVI. See the useful article, 'Pueden los Ultras Copar Santiago' in *Que Pasa*, 12 April 1973. To the considerable annoyance of the Communists, the industrial wing of the MIR–FTR made steady gains among construction workers. In elections for the construction syndicate in Antofagasta in February 1973, for example, the FTR polled more than twice as many votes as the Communists (who had formerly controlled the union directorate), coming a close second to the Socialists. See *El Rebelde*, 27 February 1973
4 Printed in *Tarea Urgente* No 1, 16 February 1973
5 Interview in *El Rebelde*, 27 February 1973
6 This meeting was arranged by the *Organización de Cristianos por el Socialismo*, whose secretary-general, Martín Gárate, declared that 'either a sinister minority will set up a dictatorship, or the people will conquer power to govern freely'. *El Rebelde*, 19 February 1973
7 The Communist press alleged, on the other hand, that the 'July 16th Commando' was also responsible for armed robberies in Santiago designed to finance an uprising against the government. See *El Siglo*, 21 July 1972
8 See, for example, Roberto Pintos's article in *El Siglo*, 18 July 1971, and José Rodriguez Elizondo, 'Mitología de la ultraizquierda' in *Principios*, May–June 1971
9 *El Mercurio*, 3 February 1972
10 Supplement to *El Rebelde*, 27 February 1973
11 Enriquez' oration at the funeral of Luciano Cruz. Reprinted in *Punto Final*, 31 August 1971
12 Reprinted as an appendix to Debray, *Conversations with Allende*, op cit
13 *Punto Final*, 8 June 1971

14 *Punto Final,* 9 November 1971
15 Bautista Van Schouwen's speech on the death of the Brazilian revolutionary, Carlos Lamarca. See *Punto Final,* 12 October 1971
16 This document was leaked to *Ercilla.* See the issue of 1 September 1971
17 *Punto Final,* 27 October 1970
18 Ibid
19 *La Prensa,* 1 September 1971
20 See Saavedra, Patricio, *La Cuestión Mapuche* (Santiago 1971)
21 *La Prensa,* 28 February 1972

CHAPTER SIX

1 Fuentealba, 'Analísis de la Situación política del Pais', reprinted in *Política y Espiritu* (Santiago September 1971)
2 On the constitutional issues involved, see Carlos Cruz-Coke, 'Debate Sobre Despacho de la Reforma Constitucional' in *El Mercurio,* 27 February 1972
3 *El Mercurio,* 17 December 1971
4 *El Siglo,* 11 April 1971
5 *El Mercurio,* 14 April 1971
6 For further examples of how the Statute was contravened, see 'La Burla de las garantías constitucionales' in *Portada* No 35 (special issue) pp32–5. See also Tomás P. McHale's valuable little book, *El Frente de la Libertad de Expresión* (Ediciones Portada, Santiago 1972)
7 See *La Prensa,* 21 April 1972
8 This was disclosed through the private investigations of a Christian Democrat deputy, José Monares. See *La Prensa,* 24 July 1972
9 *La Nación,* 9 September 1971
10 The government planned to launch a savage publicity campaign against this fund, but this was made impossible after *El Mercurio* divulged its intentions on 1 December 1971
11 See 'Alessandri rompe su silencio' in *Que Pasa,* 12 October 1972
12 At the advice of the American economic mission led by Edwin W. Kemmerer, whose visit had been requested by President Emiliano Figueroa. The Contraloría's historical predecessor was the Tribunal Mayor de Cuentas, founded by Bernardo O'Higgins. In Allende's time, the Contraloría had a staff of about 1,500.
13 *El Mercurio,* 13 July 1972
14 See 'Corte Suprema Respondió al Ministro de Justicia' in *El Mercurio,* 19 July 1972. For Tapia's reply, see *El Mercurio,* 21 July 1972
15 See Moss, Robert, 'Allende's Chile' in *Encounter,* August 1972
16 *Ercilla,* 18 October 1972
17 See *Que Pasa,* 19 October 1972

18   *La Prensa*, 16 October 1972
19   'Informe Confidencial del MAPU' published in *El Mercurio*,
     1 March 1973
20   Ibid

CHAPTER SEVEN

1   There is now a vast literature on the military and politics in Latin
     America. Good basic studies include: Johnson, John J.
     (ed) *The Role of the Military in Underdeveloped Countries* (Prince-
     ton 1962); Lieuwen, Edward, *Generals versus Presidents* (1965);
     Nun, José, 'The Middle-Class Military Coup' in Veliz, Claudio
     (ed) *The Politics of Conformity in Latin America* (1967) and
     Stepan, Alfred, *The Military in Politics: Changing Patterns in
     Brazil* (Princeton 1971). On Chile, see Joxe, Alain, *Las Fuerzas
     Armadas en el Sistema Político de Chile* (Santiago 1970) and
     Polloni, Alberto, *Las Fuerzas Armadas de Chile en la Vida
     Nacional* (Santiago 1972)
2   *El Rebelde*, 6 November 1972
3   *La Aurora de Chile*, 3 November 1972
4   *Punto Final*, 21 November 1972
5   *Ercilla*, 15 November 1972
6   See Bicheno, Hugh, 'Anti-Parliamentary Themes in Chilean His-
     tory: 1920–70' in Medhurst, K. (ed), *Allende's Chile* (1972)
     and Nunn, F. M., *Chilean Politics 1920–31: The Honourable
     Mission of the Armed Forces* (University of New Mexico 1970)
7   See Rojas, Robinson, 'Que piensan las fuerzas armadas' in *Causa
     Marxista–Leninista*, July–August 1971
8   See, for example, Stepan, Alfred and Einaudi, Luigi R., *Latin
     American Institutional Development: Changing Military Perspec-
     tive in Peru and Brazil* (RAND Corporation 1971)
9   See Labarca, Eduardo, *Chile al Rojo*, op cit
10   *PEC*, 20 October 1972
11   Ibid
12   See 'Canales habla claro' in *Que Pasa*, 28 September 1972
13   *El Mercurio*, 7 May 1970
14   *PEC*, 20 October 1972
15   *El Mercurio*, 15 December 1970
16   *El Mercurio*, 3 March 1972
17   *Ercilla*, 29 November 1972. The television interview was with
     Raquel Correa on Channel 13.
18   On Faivovich's career, see 'Intendentes revuelven el gallinero' in
     Que Pasa, 11 January 1973
19   *El Mercurio*, 15 and 18 January 1973
20   *Ercilla*, 17 January 1973
21   *El Mercurio*, 26 February 1973

22   *El Siglo*, 27 February 1973, following General Prats's appearance
     on 'A esta hora se improvisa'.

CHAPTER NINE

1   For an interesting account, see Claudio Rodriguez, 'La Masacre del
    Tacna' in *PEC*, 6 July 1973
2   See *El Mercurio* (international edition), 6–12 August 1973
3   See the interview with General Leigh in *Que Pasa*, 30 August 1973
4   *El Mercurio*, 23 August 1973
5   The Chilean armed forces (counting some 26,000 Carabineros)
    numbered only about 74,000 men, and the army had little training
    in counter-guerrilla operations.
6   Jaguaribe, Helio, *Political Development* (New York 1973), pp500–1

Select Bibliography

Allende Gossens, Salvador, *Nuestro Camino al Socialismo* (Buenos Aires 1971)

Ampuero, Raul, *El Pueblo en la Defensa Nacional* (Santiago 1971)

Angell, Alan, *Politics and the Labour Movement in Chile* (1972)

Bardón, Alvara, et al, *Itinerario de una Crisis* (Santiago 1972)

Barria, Jorge, *El Movimiento Obrero en Chile* (Santiago 1972)

Bourne, Richard, *Political Leaders of Latin America* (Harmondsworth 1969)

Cademartori, José, *La Economía Chilena* (Santiago 1968)

Canihuante, Gustavo, *La Revolución Chilena* (Santiago 1971)

Castillo, Jaime, *Las Fuentes de la Democracia Cristiana* (3rd edition, Santiago 1972)

Chamudes, Marcos, *Chile: Una Advertencia Americana* (Santiago 1972)

Clissold, Stephen, *Latin America: New World, Third World* (1972)

Corvalán, Luis, *Camino de Victoria* (Santiago 1971)

Debray, Régis, *Conversations with Allende* (1972)

—*Prison Writings* (1973)

Dowling, Jorge, *Religión, Chamanismo y Mitología mapuches* (Santiago 1971)

Encina, Francisco, *Historia de Chile* (Santiago 1949)

Eyzaguirre, Jaime, *Historia Constitucional de Chile* (Santiago 1952)

Feinberg, Richard E., *The Triumph of Allende* (New York 1972)

Frank, Andre Gunder, *Capitalism and Underdevelopment in Latin America* (New York 1967)

Garcia, Miguel, *Relato de un Brigadista* (Santiago 1971)

Gil, Federico, *The Political System of Chile* (Boston 1966)

Gurriaran, José Antonio, *Caerá Allende?* (Barcelona 1973)

Halperin, Ernst, *Nationalism and Communism in Chile* (Cambridge, Mass 1965)

Horne, Alistair, *Small Earthquake in Chile* (1972)

Huneeus, Pablo, et al, *El Costo Social de la Dependencia Ideológica* (Santiago 1973)

Jarpa, Sergio Onofre, *Creo en Chile* (Santiago 1973)

Jobet, Julio César, *El Partido Socialista de Chile*, 2 vols, (Santiago 1971)

Kaufman, Robert R., *The Politics of Land Reform in Chile 1950–1970* (Cambridge, Mass 1972)

Labarca, Eduardo, *Chile al Rojo* (Santiago 1971)

—*Corvalán 27 Horas* (Santiago 1972)

Labrousse, Alain, *L'Expérience Chilienne* (Paris 1972)

Laferrte, Elias, *Vida de un Comunista* (Santiago 1961)

Lamour, Catherine, *Le Pari Chilien* (Paris 1972)

MacHale, Tomás, P., *El Frente de la Libertad de Expresión* (Santiago 1972)

—et al, *Visión Crítica de Chile* (Santiago 1972)

Medhurst, Kenneth (ed), *Allende's Chile* (1972)

Moss, Robert, 'Allende's Chile', *Encounter* (August 1972)

—'The Santiago Model' *Conflict Studies Nos 30 and 31* (1973)

—*Urban Guerrillas* (1972)

Mourao, Gerardo Mello, *Frei y la Revolución Latinoamericana* (Santiago 1966)

Musalem, José, *Crónica de un Fracaso* (Santiago 1973)

Orrego, Claudio, *El Paro Nacional* (Santiago 1972)

Ossa, Juan Luis, *Nacionalismo Hoy* (Santiago 1972)

—*Participación para una Nueva Sociedad* (Santiago 1972)

—*El Pensamiento Económico del Gobierno de Allende* (Santiago 1971)

—*El Pensamiento Politico y Teorico del Partido Socialista* (Santiago 1972)

Pérez de Arce, Hermógenes, *Comentarios Escogidos* (Santiago 1973)

Petras, James, *Politics and Social Forces in Chilean Development* (Berkeley, Calif 1970)

Pike, Frederick, *Chile and the United States 1880–1962* (University of Notre Dame Press 1963)

Pinto, Aníbal, *Chile: Una Economía Difícil* (Fondo de Cultura, Mexico 1964)

—et al, *Chile Hoy* (Siglo Veintiuno, Mexico 1971)

Polloni, Colonel Alberto, *Las Fuerzas Armadas de Chile en le Vida Nacional* (Santiago 1972)

Prats Gonzalez, General Carlos, *Benjamin Vicuña Mackenna y las Glorias de Chile* (Santiago 1972)

Recabarren, *El Pensamiento de Luis Emilio Recabarren* (Santiago 1971)

Rodriguez Grez, Pablo, *Entre la Democracia y la Tirania* (Santiago 1971)

Saavedra, Alejandro, *La Cuestion Mapuche* (Santiago 1971)

Saenz, Orlando, *Chile, un País én Quiebra* (Santiago 1973)

Stepan, Alfred, *The Military in Politics: Changing Patterns in Brazil* (Princeton, NJ 1971)

Stevenson, John, *The Chilean Popular Front* (Philadelphia 1942)

Universidad Católica de Chile, Instituto de Economía, *Análisis de la Economía Chilena 1971–1972* (Santiago 1972)

Universidad de Chile, Instituto de Economía, *La Economía Chilena en 1971* (Santiago 1972)

Universidad de Chile, 'Taller de Coyuntura', *Comentarios Sobre la Situación Económica* Nos 1–4 (Santiago 1971–3)

Valdés, Jaime, *La 'Clase' Dorada (o el Gobierno Secreto de la UP)* (Santiago 1973)

Varas, Florencia, *Conversaciones con Viaux* (Santiago 1972)

Zammit, J. Ann (ed), *The Chilean Road to Socialism* (University of Sussex 1973)

Index